MERCEDES SL SERIES

Other Titles in the Crowood AutoClassics Series

MERCEDES SL SERIES

The Complete Story

Brian Laban

First published in 1992 by
The Crowood Press Ltd
Ramsbury, Marlborough
Wiltshire SN8 2HR

© The Crowood Press Ltd 1992

British Library Cataloguing in Publication Data

A catalogue record for this book is available from the British
Library.

ISBN   1 85223 595 0

Picture Credits

The majority of the illustrations in this book were kindly
supplied by The Motoring Picture Library, Beaulieu.

Typeset by Chippendale Type Ltd., Otley, West Yorkshire.
Printed and bound in Great Britain by BPCC Hazells Ltd
Member of BPCC Ltd

Contents

THE SL FAMILY: A BRIEF HISTORY

1951 June: a delegation from Daimler-Benz attends the Le Mans 24-Hour race as a first step towards planning a return to international sports car racing.
Winter: first prototype of the new racing sports car tested by chief development engineer Rudi Uhlenhaut.

1952 March: 300SL launched as a racing coupé, with six-cylinder carburettor engine, swing-axle rear suspension and 'gullwing' doors. In May the 300SL made its racing début in the Mille Miglia; in coupé and later open-topped form, the racing 300SL won several major races including Le Mans and the Carrera Panamericana but Mercedes abandoned sports car racing before 1953.

1953 US Mercedes importer Max Hoffman asked Mercedes to build a production version of the racer and ordered 1,000 cars. Mercedes started development, based on the racing coupé.

1954 January: production version of the 300SL launched at the New York Motor Sports Show, with fuel-injected six-cylinder engine and gullwing doors. It was the fastest production sports car in the world.

1955 January: smaller, cheaper, four-cylinder 190SL (announced alongside 300SL early in 1954) finally into production after several revisions – using unitary construction and many production-sourced parts. Ran largely unchanged until 1963.
Though not strictly part of the main SL family, the W196 GP-car-based 300SLR took Mercedes back into sports car racing and dominated the season, but was at the centre of the biggest ever motor racing tragedy at Le Mans in June.

1957 March: 300SL coupé replaced by the 300SL Roadster, which was broadly similar but with a revised chassis (allowing conventional doors), improved rear suspension, and several styling changes; soft-top and removable hard-top options were offered.

1961 March: disc brakes available for the first time on the 300SL Roadster.

1963 March: completely new SL range launched with the six-cylinder 'pagoda-roof' 230SL, replacing both the 300SL and 190SL, again with soft-top and/or removable hard-top options. Automatic transmission offered for the first time as the SL range became more refined.

1966 March: 230SL uprated with larger engine to become the 250SL. Rear disc brakes replaced drums and several new safety features were incorporated, prompted by US legislation.

1967 Further capacity increase turned the 250SL into the 280SL, with option of five-speed manual gearbox and other minor changes.

1971 280SL replaced by virtually all-new third generation SL with V8 engine. Launched as the 350SL in Europe but needed a 4.5-litre engine in USA to counter mandatory emissions equipment. Bigger and better equipped car with further improved rear suspension and many more changes confirmed continuing shift up market for the SL philosophy.
Mercedes added the longer wheelbase, fixed-roof, full four-seater SLC coupé derivatives to the range, mechanically and visually very closely related to the two-plus-two seater SLs. The SLCs generally followed the SL engine options until late 1981, when they were replaced by new saloon-based coupés.

1974 With the 450SL also available in Europe since mid-1973 and 'safety bumpers' on US models, Mercedes responded to the first 'energy crisis' by reintroducing a six-cylinder SL, the new 280SL, which otherwise looked very much like its bigger brothers.

1980 With fewer worries about oil prices, Mercedes upgraded the 350SL to the 380SL and the 450SL to the alloy-engined 500SL – the last of which survived until 1989.

1985 Alongside the 500SL, the 420SL replaced the 380SL and the 300SL replaced the 280SL.

1986 The biggest of all SL engines was offered, on the US market only, in the 560SL, which featured minor bodywork changes including front and rear spoilers, and further upgraded comfort and safety equipment.

1987 February: spy pictures of a new generation SL appeared in several motoring magazines.

1989 August: last of the third-generation SLs was built for the Daimler-Benz museum.
March: the current SL range – the fourth generation – was launched, continuing the SL tradition of soft- and hard-top options but now with more sophisticated technology than ever before. The 300SL, 300SL-24 and 500SL offered two-valve and four-valve six-cylinder engines and a four-valve V8, plus five-speed manual and four- or five-speed automatic gearboxes plus world-leading engineering.

Introduction

In the years leading up to World War II European motor racing enjoyed one of its periodic 'golden ages'. From the early 1930s until the actual day when war broke out, Grand Prix racing in particular had developed into a battle of the titans. They were years marked by astonishing technical progress and by the growth of motor sport in general from a gentleman's pastime to a political tool. They were also the years when a Nazi government hungry for image-boosting propaganda poured massive annual subsidies into two German racing teams, and in so doing made them virtually invincible.

From 1934 to 1939 the Grand Prix teams from Auto-Union and Mercedes-Benz simply steamrollered the British, French and Italian opposition, with an unprecedented mixture of money and high technology. Auto-Union's rear-engined cars (as designed by Dr Porsche) won their fair share, but by far the most prolific winners were the magnificent Silver Arrows from Mercedes, which added victory after victory to an already formidable sporting record stretching back to the birth of the automobile.

Then came the war and an enforced end to the frivolities of motor racing for the duration. Daimler-Benz, parent company of the Mercedes marque, was one of the mainstays

Before World War II, Mercedes (alongside Auto-Union) dominated motor sport, with cars like this W125 streamliner as seen at Avus in 1937, and sponsorship as revealed on the driver's fairing.

of the German war machine, building a huge range of military equipment from the German equivalent of the Jeep to some of the war's finest aero engines. The huge and expensive 'Grosser' Mercedes car was also the first choice transport of the Nazi hierarchy, and such foreign dignitaries as Josef Stalin and General Franco. Not too surprisingly, the Daimler factories were made to suffer heavily for all that in repeated waves of Allied bombing.

A SPECTACULAR RECOVERY

At the end of the hostilities, many of Daimler-Benz's factories were completely destroyed, but the company's ambitions were not and as soon as they possibly could they resumed civilian production. In 1946 they built just over 200 cars; in 1947, over 1,000; in 1948, well over 5,000, and the German currency reforms in the middle of

The 300 SL took Mercedes back into the production sports car market in 1954 and gave the world a new motoring word with its 'gullwing' doors.

The SL tradition continues in the ultra-sophisticated and highly desirable current generation, including the 300SL–24.

that year finally allowed them back into a true world market. As early as 1950, they comfortably surpassed their record annual total of the pre-war years with an output of almost 34,000 cars, and they began to turn their attentions once again to motor sport.

This time there would be no bottomless pit of government money to draw on, just the company's own resources and, initially at least, the target would be one rung down from Grand Prix racing, in international sports car racing.

In 1951 Daimler-Benz sent a party of their eager-to-work racing technicians to watch the jewel in the sports car racing crown, Le

Mans; exactly one year later the racing department were back at Le Mans with a team of cars, and the new Silver Arrows finished first and second. In the same year they won the Mille Miglia and an event that many people would regard as the most gruelling road race of them all, the Carrera Panamericana.

The car that did all of that and so convincingly relaunched Mercedes' racing career was known as the 300SL – '300' for its 3-litre capacity and 'SL' for the German *Super-Licht*, or super-lightweight. It was a two-seater sports car but purely a competition model, and it was the start of a new Mercedes racing dynasty which grew through the even more specialized 300SLR sports racer and the closely related W196 Grand Prix car until it was brought to a premature end by the Le Mans disaster of 1955, in which Mercedes tragically were the central players.

In 1954, Mercedes turned the 300SL into the fastest roadgoing sports car in the world and in doing so started a family of sporting Mercedes road cars which is still going strong – the SLs. In all that time there have really been very few distinct generations of SL. The original coupé with its distinctive 'gullwing' doors lasted until 1957 and its open-topped Roadster sibling, with some notable improvements in its handling and everyday practicality, kept that first generation alive until 1963. Alongside them, from 1955 to 1963, ran a smaller but still highly regarded model, the 190SL, which was based on the bare bones of Mercedes' first unit construction saloon and as such was the first SL model that was profitably mass-producable.

THE SECOND GENERATION

Replacing both the 300 Roadster and the 190s, a second generation was introduced in 1963. It was not quite the compromise it might have sounded, but more a reflection of the way the market had changed and of the new competition any Mercedes sports car now had to face. Like the 190, it used a lot of production car spin-offs and it used them well. A new rear suspension layout, for instance, saw the original 230SL widely praised as one of the best handling cars in the world. Although it was nowhere near as quick as the earlier 300s and even offered automatic transmission, it was far more refined than the original, race-bred cars and well worthy of the SL name – which was now taken to mean *Sport-Licht* or lightweight sports car.

The lightweight label was already becoming slightly dubious, but the second generation SL still had a very special character. It had a more angular design than the curvaceous older cars, and was distinguished in its hard-top versions by a 'pagoda-top' roof line. From 1963 to 1971 bigger versions of its six-cylinder engine saw it through 230, 250 and 280 guises, but as is often the way with such things, the 'improvements' were less desirable than they might have seemed at first glance. Between 230 and 280, the SL gained more weight than power, and also lost some of its handling sharpness in favour of ease of maintenance.

AND A THIRD

Meanwhile, the opposition caught up and the SL came to be seen less as a sports car and more as a stylish and luxurious sporting tourer, until in its turn it was replaced by the next new generation in 1971. This was a car that reflected growing changes in the world's attitude to cars as a whole. With new interest in safety and pollution control, the USA in particular (and that meant the biggest market-place for virtually any sporting car maker) was shaping the way cars looked and drove – with more weight and less power initially as manufacturers came to terms with the new challenges.

Yet although 'sports car' as such became rather dirty words for a while, Mercedes, while marketing the two-seater SLs as luxurious and superbly engineered tourers, still managed to keep something of the SL's sporting tradition alive, and the third generation became the most successful to date in terms of sales and profits.

These cars had started life with more powerful yet more refined V8 engines (which eventually ranged in capacity from 3.5 to 5.6 litres), but from 1974, reacting to the first oil crisis of 1973 and a European market opening for a more economical SL, Mercedes

'Father of the SLs': the great engineer Rudi Uhlenhaut, seen here at the German GP in 1938.

again supplemented the range with six-cylinder models, and those sixes and V8s survived all the way to 1989.

THE CURRENT FAMILY

The year 1989 saw the launch of the current family of ultra-sophisticated, bristling-with-technology SLs, the V8-engined 500, and the six-cylinder 300s in both 12- and 24-valve form. Mercedes launched these cars as 'a state of the art approach to the design of a luxury sports car' and went to great lengths to emphasize the heritage of all the SLs that went before. The design team which worked on the car for some ten years declared that it was 'the most difficult and challenging task that we have ever faced', but at the end of it all, Mercedes was adamant in describing the SL as 'once again a true sports car'. Not every tester agreed entirely with that description, but very few thought the car less than brilliant by whatever definition.

In so many ways the SLs are unique cars. Some people would argue that only the very first were true sports cars, though nobody could argue that any of them was less than sporty. From the first they were developed by the men who shaped Mercedes' racing technology, and ever since then they have been flagships for Mercedes' technical excellence. They are expensive without being blatantly ostentatious, bought more for their hewn-from-solid mechanical reliability than for a spectacular image, yet they retain a pleasing degree of the old iron fist within the velvet glove. Mercedes' post-war reputation as a manufacturer with a sporting heritage would have been a lot poorer without them.

1 Daimler-Benz: A Sporting Heritage

If one car in motoring history could be said to have broken away from nineteenth-century 'horseless carriage' thinking and set the scene for the 'modern' automobile as we would recognize it today, it was the car built by Wilhelm Maybach for the Daimler Motoren-Gesellschaft in 1901.

Maybach was helped and supported by Paul Daimler, son of the firm's founder Gottlieb who had died in March 1900. The car they designed had a pressed steel frame when most competitors were still using wood with some token steel reinforcement; it had mechanically operated inlet valves, while others were still relying on suction; it had Maybach's pioneering spray-type carburettor; it had a gated gear-change to take away some of the guesswork of everyone else's rough-and-ready systems; and it had a honeycomb radiator rather than the earlier and cruder finned tubes. Even its unusually low build was recognizably more 'modern' than anything that had gone before.

The car had been commissioned by one Emil Jellinek, an Austrian trader-become-banker who was also now his country's

The name 'Mercedes' was born with this four-cylinder 35hp car built by Wilhelm Maybach for Daimler in 1901.

Emil Jellinek, Austrian Consul-General in Nice, sporting motorist and Daimler agent, who needed a new name for a new car in a sensitive market-place.

Mercédès Jellinek, the ten-year-old daughter whose name became one of the most famous marques in history.

Consul-General in Nice. Jellinek had bought one of the earlier Daimler Phönix cars in 1897 and subsequently, through his enthusiastic promotion of the firm's products among his wealthy society friends and business associates, had become (albeit unofficially at first) Daimler's first agent on the French Riviera.

Jellinek was also an ethusiastic sporting driver and had used his Phönix to good effect at the Nice speed trials – using his elder daughter's name as a pseudonym. He asked Daimler for the new model after he began to run into a degree of sales resistance to the older ones, which were suddenly being seen as top-heavy and too short in the wheelbase – an impression unfortunately generated when the driver of one was killed on the Nice – La Turbie hillclimb.

Then, having encouraged Daimler and Maybach to design and build the new car, Jellinek negotiated the rights to sell it as sole agent for France, Belgium, Austro-Hungary and the USA. There was a minor catch, however, in so far as Panhard already had sole rights to sell Daimler cars in France, but Jellinek's diplomatic and trading skills had already come up with an answer to that. For his part, he would undertake to Daimler to sell the first thirty-six examples of Maybach's seminal new design, and to get around the problems with Panhard he would give it a new name – after the same ten-year-old daughter whose name he had appropriated for his racing pseudonym.

The girl was called Mercédès.

THE NAME STICKS

Within a year (although strictly speaking it was only legally necessary for Jellinek and Daimler to use the alternative name in France, in deference to Panhard), the brilliant 1901 Daimler had become almost universally known as the Mercédès. During 1901 a team of the 5.9-litre 35hp cars were raced in Nice and completely overshadowed all the opposition; thereafter, both the Mercédès name and the company's reputation for building outstanding racing cars were firmly established.

PIONEERS

With its near neighbours Benz, Daimler was among the oldest and most respected pioneers of the industry. When the two names amalgamated as Daimler-Benz in the 1920s and became makers of the Mercedes-Benz car, the new company quickly formed a reputation that was even bigger than the sum of its parts. Strangely, however, the two founders of the industry, Gottlieb Daimler and Karl Benz, had never so much as met although they lived and worked barely sixty miles away from each other close to Stuttgart.

Daimler, born in 1834, had served an apprenticeship as a gunsmith before moving via a polytechnic course into the engineering industry and eventually, in 1872, to work as technical director for the Deutz Gas Engine Works. He helped Deutz to grow dramatically while Gustav Otto, the Deutz director who had invented the atmospheric engine, went on to develop his four-stroke engine, which was being tested by the autumn of 1876.

Daimler and Otto, however, in spite of working for the same company and towards much the same goals, could rarely agree with each other on which engine held the best promise for the long-term future. Otto and Deutz were set on big and clumsy industrial engines while Daimler saw the future in smaller, lighter petrol engines. In 1881, after a final disagreement, Daimler left Deutz and Otto.

He set up shop in Canstatt with Wilhelm Maybach, who was his long-time friend and who had been his chief designer at Deutz. Refining Otto's principles and finally overcoming numerous early failures, the two began to build their own single-cylinder petrol engines. In November 1885, Daimler fitted one of these half-horsepower units into what looked like a heavy, boneshaker bicycle with additional stabilizer wheels, just to prove that it could move under its own power. That done, in 1886 he fitted a 1.1hp engine into a four-wheeler chassis adapted from a horse-drawn carriage, with belt- and gear-drive to the rear wheels. In so doing, Daimler created the first four-wheeled motor car.

For some years, however, most of Daimler's engines went into small boats, railway carriages and even some early airships, or into factories for stationary use.

Simultaneously, he was designing a lighter and more powerful V-twin engine, and in 1889 he showed it off at the Paris Exhibition, in his *Stahlradwagen*, or steel-wheeled car. Panhard et Levassor bought the rights to manufacture the engine in France and later supplied units to Peugeot.

Expanding his company and attracting outside investors, Daimler formed Daimler Motoren-Gesellschaft in November 1890 and promptly fell out with most of his partners. In 1892 he left with Maybach and set up a small workshop in a disused hotel in Canstatt, where Maybach invented the spray carburettor and the two of them developed a high-speed in-line twin-cylinder engine which they called the Phönix. They also designed a rather heavy and clumsy belt-driven car in which to put it.

RECONCILIATION

In fact, they never built a complete car at the

old Hotel Hermann, but instead made up their differences and went back to the original company late in 1895. The other partners had built maybe a dozen cars in Daimler and Maybach's absence, but now Daimler was set to expand dramatically. First a commercial vehicle line was launched in 1896 (alongside the thriving train, boat and aeroplane lines) and then the Phönix car was introduced in 1897 with front engine, chain drive and four-speed gearbox. This was, of course, the car that brought them into contact with Jellinek.

In 1900, the year in which Gottlieb Daimler died, the company moved their car operation to Unterturkheim, from where the first 300SLs would emerge a little over half a century later and which is still the company's headquarters.

Following on the success of the first Mercédès they positively flowered, with Maybach as technical director and Jellinek too now on the board.

Inevitably, they went racing. In 1903 they entered three specially prepared 90hp cars to represent Germany in the prestigious Gordon Bennett Cup races in Ireland, but the cars were destroyed even before the event, in a fire at the factory. Daimler hastily borrowed and prepared three privately-owned 9.2-litre 60hp models and one of them, driven by Camille Jenatzy (the bearded 'Red Devil' and former world speed record holder), won the race.

While the company built better and better production cars (and other makes around the world from Fiat in Italy to Locomobile in America copied them more or less blatantly),

From the earliest days, sporting success was everything, and victory for Camille Jenatzy on one of the hastily prepared 60hp racers in the 1903 Gordon-Bennett Cup in Ireland added to a formidable reputation.

The Mercédès 1914 GP car brought the marque back into racing after a short absence, with advanced, lightweight design and to immediate success.

they also carried on winning races whenever they chose to enter. In 1908 Christian Lautenschlager won the French GP for a team that already had all the hallmarks of Neubauer's later organization, with forward planning, discipline and attention to the tiniest detail. The car won with a fairly 'ordinary' 12.8-litre, 135bhp engine, partly because of the excellence of its chassis which again foreshadowed even the concept of the original 300SL racers.

On the next of their occasional racing blitzkriegs, in the 1914 GP, the new 4½-litre Mercédès finished first, second and third. Again the teamwork helped, but the cars were also far more advanced than their competitors. The engine incorporated lessons

of light weight and high power that Daimler had learned from building aero engines, the chassis was as effective as could be, and Daimler had even made every effort to keep the car as low, compact and air-cheating as possible. It also won at Indianapolis in 1915.

THE OTHER HALF

Between 1902 and 1905 Mercédès cars also held the land-speed record on half a dozen occasions, at speeds ranging from 65.8mph (105.9kph) to 109.7mph (176.5kph), but in this discipline at least they were about to be overshadowed by Benz, who had struggled initially with their production cars, and in spite of some successes had generally had to bow to Daimler when they clashed on the racing scene.

Of course, both companies had grown up almost side by side. Karl Benz was born in 1844 and ten years Gottlieb Daimler's junior, but by common consensus he beat his neighbour by just a few months in building the first practicable motor car – albeit a three-wheeler compared to Daimler's four.

Like Daimler he had had a polytechnic education before moving into engineering, and then setting up on his own in Mannheim in 1872. By 1880, having survived near bankruptcy and with his wife Bertha's encouragement, he had built a two-stroke engine – avoiding a clash with Otto's four-stroke patents. By 1884 Benz und Cie: Rheinische Gasmotorenfabrik were working on a powerful, lightweight four-stroke.

Early in 1885 his engine worked, and late in the year he fitted it into a three-wheeler chassis with tiller steering and chain drive. Where Daimler would motorize a heavy horse-drawn carriage, Benz built his elegant little chassis from scratch, with as little weight as possible and showing a fine understanding of the fundamental problem of motorized transport both then and now. His horizontally-mounted engine had electric ignition and produced more than 2hp; the whole vehicle was already far more practical than the first Daimler, but it was in Karl Benz's nature to try constantly to improve things and that is just what he did for the next couple of years. His success was proved when Bertha drove the car and her two sons on the 100-mile (160km) round trip from Mannheim to Pforzheim and back in August 1888, and again shortly after when Karl drove 200 miles (320km) to show his vehicle at the International Exhibition in Munich.

From 1887 he underlined his right to be called the father of the motor car when he offered copies of his vehicle for sale. Parisian bicycle dealer Emile Roger (who also built Benz stationary engines under licence for France) bought the first in 1887, and in effect became the world's first motor car dealer.

Again like Daimler, Benz expanded his company with outside backing, built a number of three-wheelers up to 1892 and then launched his first four-wheeler, the Viktoria. That sold in considerable numbers and the lighter, cheaper Velo, introduced in 1894, turned Benz und Cie into the first real volume car builder. Benz's 181 sales in 1896 were more than the combined total of all other car makers in Europe and the USA – several of whom were only in business anyway by virtue of copying Benz's designs. By the turn of the century he had delivered over 2,000 cars and, commercially at least, was a long way ahead of Daimler.

Then it all started to go wrong, ironically in part because the man who had invented the motor car was happy to improve the old but reluctant to develop the new. In another parallel to Daimler's career, he walked out of his own company in 1903, went back in 1904, and then left for good in 1906 with his two sons, to found C. Benz und Sohne in nearby Ladenburg.

RACING AND RECORDS

Those left behind, and notably the new chief designer Hans Nibel, included a number of racing enthusiasts, and between 1903 and 1914 Benz were regularly seen in competition. Their three cars finished second, third and fifth to Jenatzy's Mercédès in the 1908 GP, and in 1909 Victor Héméry took the land speed record at Brooklands with a speed of 125.9mph (202.6kph). That was in the first example of the most famous Benz of them all, the massive but carefully lightened and streamlined 21-litre, 200bhp *Blitzen* Benz. In 1911, Bob Burman raised the record to 141.4mph (227.6kph) at Daytona, and Benz even sold a few cars with the *Blitzen* engine for use on the road!

After the interruption of World War I, Daimler and Benz renewed their rivalries for sales and competition success. On the production front, Benz continued with conventional and worthy, but largely uninspiring extensions of pre-war designs; Daimler soon underlined their sporting character by introducing the first ever supercharged production cars in 1921 – having proved the supercharger in competition when Max Sailer won the Coppa Florio with a blown Mercédès 28/95 which he had driven all the way from Stuttgart!

A couple of years later Daimler brought supercharging to the GP circuits, and over the next few years created a string of magnificent supercharged sports cars and competition sports cars, with four, six and even eight cylinders and capacities from 4 litres to 6.2 litres. The four-cylinder cars were especially effective, and won both the Targa and Coppa Florio races in 1924.

By this time Paul Daimler had retired, and from 1922 Daimler had a new chief engineer – one Ferdinand Porsche. It was Porsche who designed the new, supercharged, overhead-camshaft six-cylinder engines, and these cars gave the Mercédès name the most glamorous of images in the mid-1920s.

Benz, meanwhile, were going down a different revolutionary route in motor sport. In 1923, at the Italian GP at Monza, they entered two 2-litre cars known as the *Tropfenwagen*. Their six-cylinder engines were orthodox enough, but they sat behind the driver, in a cigar-like streamlined shell spoiled only by the hole for the driver and a strange curved radiator protruding behind. They also had swing-axle rear suspension, another first for a racing car. The *Tropfenwagen* was not a particularly successful concept in either single- or two-seater form, but it showed that Benz did still have a spark of originality.

Mercédès raced and won in the toughest of events; this is Graf Masetti in the Targa Florio in Sicily in 1922.

Alfred Neubauer, later racing team manager and one of the instigators of the SL programme, was one of the victorious team in the 1924 Targa Florio.

TOWARDS A MERGER

On the other hand, Benz also had financial problems and the German market was very weak. By 1923 they were already talking about the obvious solution of merging with their major rivals, Daimler.

The final trigger was the way Benz was financed, with the majority shareholding held by a notorious company speculator, Jacob Schapiro. Schapiro also hamstrung Benz in other ways through his interests in their suppliers, until eventually Benz's financial director, in league with the Deutsche Bank, gradually and cleverly bought up enough of Schapiro's holdings to take control

of Benz. The same bank also owned a substantial share of Daimler, and from there on the merger took its natural and sensible course. The two companies signed a declaration of mutual interests in May 1924 and on 1 July 1926 completed a full merger.

The new company was called Daimler-Benz AG and was headed by the Benz financial director who had initiated the amalgamation, Wilhelm Kissel. Also on the new board were Hans Nibel from Benz, Ferdinand Porsche and Fritz Nallinger from Daimler. When Nibel died prematurely in 1934, Nallinger would become engineering director of Daimler-Benz, and in 1952 it would be Nallinger who was one of the mainstays of the

300SL project – with his chief assistant Rudi Uhlenhaut.

After the merger, Daimler-Benz combined the three-pointed star which had graced Mercédès cars since 1909 and the laurel wreath of Benz, to form the badge that is still familiar today. The cars would be called Mercedes-Benz, having shed the Fran-cophile accents inherited from the young Miss Jellinek in 1901.

The combined operation was rationalized and it flourished, but the cars quickly became almost exclusively Mercedes. Unterturkheim remained the headquarters and Sindelfingen became the main body plant. In the late 1920s and early 1930s two car lines ran side by side – the bread-and-butter six- and eight-cylinder side-valve touring models designed by Nibel, and the super-sporting line designed by Porsche, culminating in the legendary, supercharged SS, SSK and SSKL

models. The latter versions of these sold in small numbers at staggering prices but gener-ated massive prestige through competition success, and the SSKL was in effect the works racing model.

Porsche moved on in 1928 en route to Auto-Union, and was succeeded as chief designer by Nibel, who therefore oversaw the astonishing racing successes of the big supercharged cars, from the 1929 Tourist Trophy to the 1931 Mille Miglia, and even some extraordinarily near misses for stripped SSKs against pukka GP machinery at circuits as different as Monaco and the Nurburgring. However, in 1931, against a background of slump in the industry, Mercedes withdrew from sports car racing and consolidated their commercial position by starting a fine and long running series of smaller saloon cars with the 170, which would even see them back into production after World War II.

Caracciola and Werner in their SS led a Mercedes 1–2–3 in the German GP for sports cars at the Nurburgring in 1928.

The aggressively sporty, short-chassis 1929 SSK was typical of the kind of supercharged high-performance model with which Mercedes challenged Bentley in the 1920s and 1930s.

The lone white Mercedes of Caracciola and Werner at Le Mans in 1930 – fast enough but the odds were too great.

RACING FOR GERMANY

There was a final and spectacular racing fling before the war, of course, when Daimler-Benz returned to GP racing for the new formula of 1934. The company committed themselves to building a Mercedes-Benz GP car as early as March 1933, and only after that did they find a new and generous backer in the shape of Adolf Hitler's National Socialist government. Daimler-Benz and Hitler were both interested in motor sport to demonstrate superiority of a sort, but the superiorities were subtly different . . .

Either way, the government was willing to back whichever bit of the German motor industry could win the most prestige through motor racing, and in the end that boiled down to a massively subsidized head-to-head battle between the new Mercedes designed by Nibel and the new Auto-Unions designed by Porsche. Porsche produced his mid-engined cars and Nibel produced the front-engined W25, which produced over 350bhp from its supercharged straight-eight engine while

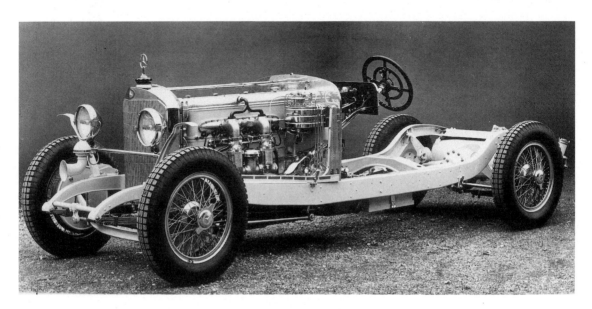

Engineering on the grand scale; the bare chassis of the supercharged 1929 38/250hp SS.

*Added lightness; the chassis of the supercharged six-cylinder SSK racer of 1928
was honeycombed with holes in case 7.1 litres and 300hp was not enough.*

*There were smaller sporty cars too, like the 1.7-litre, four-cylinder, two-seater
170V roadster of 1936 . . .*

. . . and even this rear-engined 1.5-litre four-cylinder 150H experiment of 1935 . . .

. . . but the mainstream was still in big, powerful and very expensive cars like this 1936 540K Cabriolet.

Immediately before World War II, Mercedes used a virtually unlimited racing budget to develop world-beating technology, but the awesome W125 could only finish second to Auto-Union here at the 1937 Donington GP.

still being under the 1,653lb (750kg) weight limit which defined the formula. After early problems with a surplus of power over roadholding, the W25s dominated GP racing for 1935, but gave the best places to Auto-Union in 1936, even though they had grown to 4.7 litres and almost 500bhp. That all left the Italian, French and British opposition looking pathetically outmoded.

In 1937 Daimler-Benz replied with the stunning Mercedes-Benz W125, with 646bhp and a chassis which could handle most of it. Its brilliance lay in using a relatively soft but well-controlled suspension on an ultra-stiff tubular frame. Much of the thinking came from the young development engineer who had joined Daimler-Benz in 1931 and joined the racing department late in 1936 — the department run by Max Sailer and Fritz Nallinger since the untimely death of Nibel in 1934. The young man's name was Rudi Uhlenhaut, and come 1952 he would be the father of the SL, being directly involved with it right into the mid-1970s and the third generation.

After one year in which the W125 dominated, the GP formula changed to limit the size of supercharged engines to just 3 litres and supposedly to contain speeds. However, the V12-engined Mercedes-Benz W154 with two-stage supercharging, and its 1939 successor the W163, comprehensively destroyed that theory with virtually 200mph (320kph) performance and almost total control of the sport. From 1937 to 1939 the team, managed by the legendary Alfred Neubauer, won nineteen out of the twenty-eight GPs they contested.

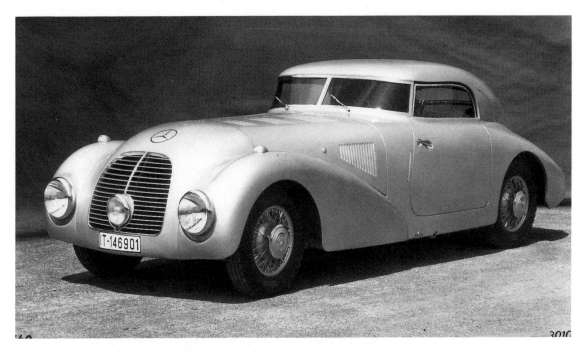

Racing sports cars were part of the scene even before the war; this is a special-bodied 540K from 1939.

When World War II interrupted, all that staggering technical development and frighteningly single-minded backing stopped, of course, but when the War was over there was enough spirit and bomb-damaged substance left at Daimler-Benz for the company to start again and put itself back together. There were also still people like Nallinger, Neubauer and Uhlenhaut, and there was the ambition to show that what they had done so many times before they could do again. By 1951 they were looking for a way to go racing and the path to the SL family was ahead . . .

2 Starting Point: Developing the Competition 300SLs

SOMETHING TO FOLLOW

In 1930 the entry for Le Mans was the smallest in the history of the race, with just seventeen cars, but it promised one of the most dramatic confrontations yet seen in the classic event. For the first time ever a works Mercedes appeared on the entry list for the 24-Hour 'GP d'Endurance', to be driven by Mercedes' massively talented 'Rainmaster' Rudi Caracciola and veteran driver Christian Werner.

Daimler-Benz's lone white SS would face no less than five of Britain's mighty Bentleys – the cars which had won the Le Mans race four times in the seven runnings since it was created in 1923, and whose victories included the last three races in succession. The Bentleys for 1930 included three of the well-proven Speed Sixes entered by the works, and two of the cars that W.O. Bentley himself disliked so much – the supercharged 4½-litre 'Blower' model, built and privately entered by the Birkin/Paget team. The singleton Mercedes was even bigger than the formidable Bentleys (which Ettore Bugatti once described as 'the fastest lorries in the world'): a huge supercharged 7.1-litre model with massive Roots supercharger which gave it around 225bhp and a blood-curdling scream when the blower was on full song.

Even so, on paper this might have had the hallmarks of a totally one-sided fight, but the reputation of Mercedes and especially of their number one driver, Caracciola, suggested it could be a mighty battle; and so it proved.

Caracciola led the field away in the screaming white Mercedes but was passed within a few laps by Birkin's Blower Bentley, even though the latter had already shed

Last time out at Le Mans, with Caracciola and the big white SS in 1930. Now it was time to try again.

Rudi Caracciola, the racing genius who was still on the Mercedes racing team after the war.

a rear tyre tread. When Birkin's tyre finally burst, Caracciola retook the lead, hounded constantly by the other Bentleys. Dunfee, his first pursuer, ended his chase in a sand-bank, and team patron Woolf Barnato took up the pursuit and eased into the lead while the Mercedes was in its pit.

Over the next few hours, the lead changed back and forth between the two marques until they approached the half-way mark, when the outnumbered but by no means outpaced Mercedes was put out of the race by what was reported to be an electrical failure. The Barnato/Kidston Bentley went on to win Bentley's fourth Le Mans in a row and what proved to be the marque's last, because shortly afterwards the works team withdrew from racing, suffering like so many others from the depression in the motor industry.

Thereafter, Caracciola's privately-entered Mercedes beat the private Bentleys (and everyone else) in the 1930 Irish GP. Another private entry repeated the works car's 1929 class win in the Tourist Trophy, and Mercedes SS, SSK and SSKL models went on to win the Mille Miglia, Avus and the European Hillclimb championship in 1930, and races including Avus, the German and Argentine GPs, the Mille Miglia and the Spa 24-Hour race in 1931, plus another European Hillclimb title.

SPORTS CARS ABANDONED . . .

They only managed second place at Le Mans in 1931 and that too was with a private entry because, like Bentley, the works team had been forced by the depression to abandon racing for the time being. When they returned, with massive backing from the new National Socialist government in the mid-1930s, they switched their attentions from sports car racing to GP racing. By the time World War II stopped all Mercedes' motor racing activity for more than a decade, the privately entered second place in 1931 remained their best ever result in the world's greatest endurance race, and the 1930 challenge to Bentley remained their one and only works participation. In the early 1950s, however, that was to change.

As late as the end of 1950 (in which year Germany was finally allowed to return to international racing), Mercedes were still rebuilding factories that had been 80 per cent flattened by wartime bombing, and production was limited to only three basic lines of frankly outdated saloon cars; for now, the management was more concerned with short-term survival than with rekindling racing glories. That, though, was not enough to stifle Mercedes' ambition, and it was already more a question of *when* Mercedes would return to racing rather than if. The answer came quickly. In 1951, with their commercial recovery convincingly under

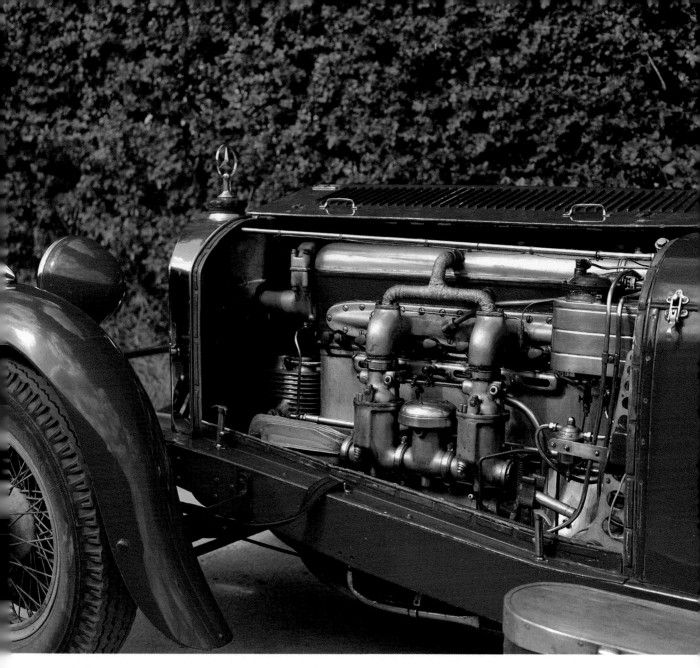

Something to live up to; the massive, supercharged, six-cylinder engine of the 1929 SSK.

way, Mercedes began openly to talk of a return to the tracks.

. . . AND REDISCOVERED

Two things above all would dictate the form of the comeback. For one, dramatic as the commercial recovery was, it was not yet quite so complete as to support a GP racing budget, and a one-off outing with the pre-

War type W163 in Argentina in February 1951 had proved that an old GP Mercedes, good as it had been in its day, could not beat a new GP Ferrari; for the other, the sport's governing body, the FIA, announced that the GP formula would change for 1954 – meaning that any new GP car for 1952 would have a short life for such a large investment. So Mercedes sensibly looked across to sports car racing as the place to prove that they were back. And of course,

*The 1951 delegation to Le Mans included Kling (standing), the rotund and
hugely respected Neubauer (with stop-watch) and Lang. Driver Hans Hermann
is seated on the left.*

that meant that they looked especially to Le Mans, which was still almost universally regarded as the greatest race in the world.

The opposition was different from that of the 1930s, with the first two races after the War (in 1949 and 1950) having been won by newcomers Ferrari and old stagers Talbot-Lago respectively. In 1951 Jaguar won the race for the first time, with their aerodynamically effective new C-Type, and one of the most exciting periods in the whole history of the race was taking shape.

A small delegation from Daimler-Benz was at Le Mans in 1951 to see that Jaguar victory and to report back to the Stuttgart hierarchy on how Mercedes should achieve their successful return to the sport they had dominated before the war. The delegation was headed by team manager Alfred Neubauer, the same rotund, autocratic but highly respected leader who had masterminded the pre-war GP domination and who had even managed that epic confrontation with the Bentleys at Le Mans back in 1930.

Neubauer had come to Daimler-Benz via Austro-Daimler and his friendship with that company's then Managing Director, Ferdinand Porsche. Neubauer had been seconded to Austro-Daimler by the army during World War I, and when the war ended Porsche retained him as production engineer and occasional competition driver with the small Porsche-designed Sascha sports cars. In 1923 Porsche moved to what was then simply Daimler and he took Neubauer with him. He raced a couple of times in Mercedes cars, with his best result a third place in the 1924 Targa Florio, but then he gave up racing to become Mercedes' racing manager. As such he became almost as famous as his star drivers until Mercedes withdrew from racing in 1955.

With Neubauer at Le Mans on the June 1951 scouting mission were two of those drivers, Karl Kling and Hermann Lang. The latter was a particularly useful observer in that before he became one of Mercedes' mainstay GP pilots in the pre-war team he had worked as a racing mechanic under Neubauer, and during the war he had been an aircraft inspector. Lang also drove alongside Fangio and Kling in one of the old W163s in that unsuccessful one-off outing in Argentina in 1951, and when the sports car programme he was now helping to plan came to fruition he would be a leading driver in that too.

In fact exactly one year later, Hermann Lang would be Mercedes' first Le Mans winner . . .

For now, he and the others were reporting back to the factory's Chief Designer Franz Roller, Technical Director Dr Fritz Nallinger (who would describe the 1952 comeback plan as 'opening the little window on motor racing') and the newly reconstituted racing department under Rudi Uhlenhaut.

BORROWING FROM PRODUCTION

Unusually for Mercedes the new sports racing car, designated type W194, was not designed from a clean sheet of paper but instead took shape around major components borrowed from an existing road car; that was quite a difference from the great days of unlimited budgets and apparently limitless technical resources.

In this case the donor car was not even a sports car (Mercedes simply did not have one in the post-war range yet) but a big and far from lightweight saloon, the 300, as introduced at the Frankfurt Show early in 1951. From it (and via the mechanically similar but somewhat sportier 300S, as launched at the Paris Show later in 1951) the sports racer would inherit its engine, transmission and basic suspension components, but all would be held together by a new and much lighter frame than the production 300s' massive cruciform of oval-section steel tubing.

It would also, of course, sit on a shorter wheelbase than either of the two offered on 300 production models (that was 120in (305cm) for the big saloons and four-door cabrio, or 114in (290cm) for the sportier two-door 300S Roadster) and it would be clothed in a sleeker, lighter shell with only two seats.

In fact, in spite of its bulk, even the six-seater 300 saloon was impressively sprightly and widely seen as a natural successor to such pre-war Mercedes masterpieces as the 500 and 540 series. Mercedes proved its abilities by using it to better the lap records set up at the Nurburgring before the war by Caracciola in the supercharged 7.1-litre SSK sports racing model. The even more lively 300S, with more power and less weight, became Germany's fastest production car, with a top speed of around 107mph (172kph).

The in-line six-cylinder engine, devised and developed by Nallinger and Uhlenhaut, with cast-iron block and aluminium alloy cylinder head, was a reasonable starting point for the sports racer. Unlike earlier series-production Mercedes engines, which tended to have long strokes and side valves, it was only slightly smaller in the bore than in the stroke (at 85.0 × 88.0mm for a capacity of 2,996cc) and had a single, duplex-chain-driven overhead camshaft operating two

The 300S was the mechanical starting point for the SL, but a very different kind of car...

overhead valves per cylinder, through finger-type rockers.

SOLID FOUNDATIONS

Using a forged steel crankshaft with seven main bearings (and with hardened journals, a new counterbalance system and a vibration damper on the nose), it was a robust engine and designed for what in 1951 passed for high revs and high specific output – another change from production tradition influenced in this case, undoubtedly, by the possibility of continuous high speeds on the extensive German autobahn system which was one of Hitler's better legacies.

It was also helped in that respect by its distinctive cylinder head and combustion chamber layout, in which the valves were not in line but were offset from each other in the flat surface of the head, and opened into a chamber which actually extended beyond the cylinder bore. That was possible

. . . even in 'sporty' coupé guise.

The massive Type 300 chassis was fine for the big saloons, but far too heavy for a planned racer.

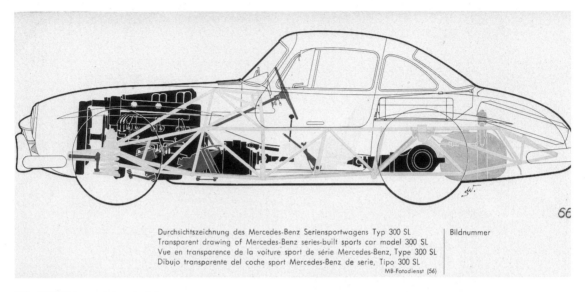

Durchsichtszeichnung des Mercedes-Benz Seriensportwagens Typ 300 SL | Bildnummer
Transparent drawing of Mercedes-Benz series-built sports car model 300 SL
Vue en transparence de la voiture sport de série Mercedes-Benz, Type 300 SL
Dibujo transparente del coche sport Mercedes-Benz de serie, Tipo 300 SL
MB-Fotodienst (56)

The 300SL's complex skeleton.

because the top face of the block was angled at some 18 degrees, and the combustion chamber was formed between the raised piston crown, the flat but angled face of the head, and the extended 'side-pocket' at the deeper side of the top of the block, into which the sparking plug projected horizontally. The overall result was to allow lots of valve area, good valve cooling, and attractively straight ports with few machining problems.

The 300 engines were novel in other ways. They were designed to run on oil which was thinner than usual to cut down on internal power losses, but that demanded very careful control of cooling. The block casting had completely open sides, covered by bolt-on plates which allowed water jacketing right down to the crankshaft centre-line, and that improved cooling for the crankcase and the upper crank bearings as well as for the linerless bores. The oil was also cooled by a tubular oil/water intercooler system integrated into the water jackets.

In the 300 saloon the engine ran with a 6.4:1 compression ratio (in deference to rather modest octane ratings in early 1950s petrol) and two downdraught Solex 40PBJC carburettors on heated manifolds. In that form it produced around 115bhp at 4,600rpm (although it was capable of running to almost 6,000rpm) and 144lb ft of torque at 2,500rpm. In the 300S, with compression increased to 7.5:1 and three rather than two carburettors, that improved to 147bhp at 5,200rpm and 166lb ft at 3,500rpm – the 'high' specific outputs being 38.4 and 49.1 bhp per litre respectively for the 300 and the 300S coupé.

PURSUIT OF POWER

For the sports racer, naturally, the racing engineers expected rather more, and that demanded a good deal of modification. Bore and stroke were left unchanged and the three-carburettor system was retained with twin fuel pumps, but the camshaft was changed, special pistons were used to raise the compression ratio to 8.0:1 and the port shapes were improved while retaining the original valve sizes. Production 300 engines used a light-alloy wet sump and the racing department were at first inclined to use just a larger version of that for the racer, but they soon adopted a dry-sump system with the scavenge pump below the pressure pump. Thus modified, power went up to 175bhp at 5,200rpm and maximum torque to 188lb ft at 4,000rpm.

To allow the lowest possible bonnet line, the engine was to be canted over at 50 degrees to the left-hand side of the car (the driver's side), which left the inlet and exhaust plumbing above the engine and the spark plugs horribly inaccessible below – at least

until fuel injection was adopted, of which more anon. It also meant that the inlet tracts were shorter than the ideal for peak power and that the exhaust manifolds had to be knitted in and out of the frame tubing, but the aerodynamic bonus obviously justified all the other hassles. The three down-draught Solex carburettors were given a single air collector which was low enough not to spoil the smooth bonnet line, open at the top and sealed by the bonnet itself when that was lowered. It picked up air from a frontal intake to give a degree of power-enhancing ram effect at high speeds.

There was enough development potential in the six-cylinder 3-litre engine with its unique cylinder-head layout for it to make the transition.

The Gullwing 300SL coupé.

(Opposite) *Lightness and efficiency were the key, and features like the spaceframe chassis and finned aluminium brakes also transferred to the production SL Series, as advertised here.*

Behind the engine was a single-plate clutch, feeding power to a four-speed, all-synchromesh manual gearbox which was virtually identical to that of the 300 saloon except that the change (a rather long lever) was on the floor rather than on the steering column! The final drive (with a choice of ratios for different circuits) was in an Elektron-alloy casing and mounted at the rear of the frame on rubber blocks. A 37½gal (170-litre) fuel tank (including a 2½gal (11-litre) reserve) was also somehow threaded into the network of tiny tubes at the rear, and above it two spare wheels would be mounted in the 'luggage compartment' behind the cockpit.

A TRUE SPACEFRAME

The frame itself was the sports car's biggest departure from the saloon. Instead of the two massive oval tubes and their heavy cross-bracing, it comprised a true space-frame, or a lattice of small diameter steel tubes almost every one of which formed the side of a triangle. Such triangles (in which the only loads are either in compression or

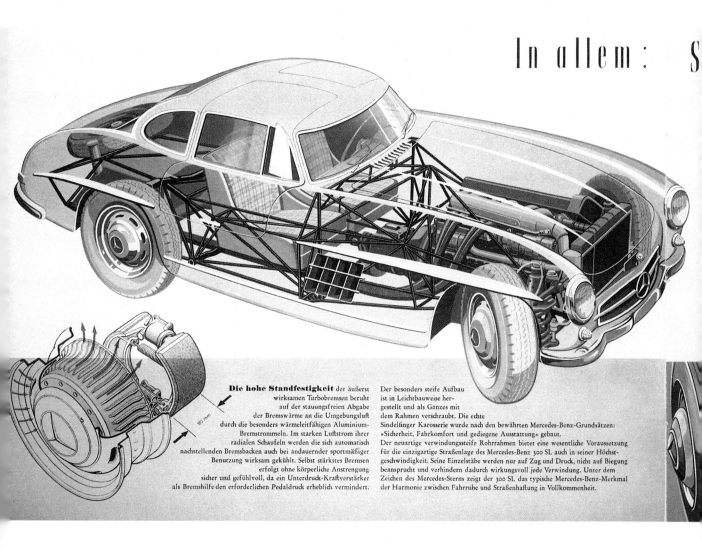

In allem: S

Die hohe Standfestigkeit der äußerst wirksamen Turbobremsen beruht auf der stauungsfreien Abgabe der Bremswärme an die Umgebungsluft durch die besonders wärmeleitfähigen Aluminium-Bremstrommeln. Im starken Luftstrom ihrer radialen Schaufeln werden die sich automatisch nachstellenden Bremsbacken auch bei andauernder sportmäßiger Benutzung wirksam gekühlt. Selbst stärkstes Bremsen erfolgt ohne körperliche Anstrengung sicher und gefühlvoll, da ein Unterdruck-Kraftverstärker als Bremshilfe den erforderlichen Pedaldruck erheblich vermindert.

Der besonders steife Aufbau ist in Leichtbauweise hergestellt und als Ganzes mit dem Rahmen verschraubt. Die echte Sindelfinger Karosserie wurde nach den bewährten Mercedes-Benz-Grundsätzen: »Sicherheit, Fahrkomfort und gediegene Ausstattung« gebaut. Der neuartige verwindungssteife Rohrrahmen bietet eine wesentliche Voraussetzung für die einzigartige Straßenlage des Mercedes-Benz 300 SL auch in seiner Höchstgeschwindigkeit. Seine Einzelstäbe werden nur auf Zug und Druck, nicht auf Biegung beansprucht und verhindern dadurch wirkungsvoll jede Verwindung. Unter dem Zeichen des Mercedes-Sterns zeigt der 300 SL das typische Mercedes-Benz-Merkmal der Harmonie zwischen Fahrruhe und Straßenhaftung in Vollkommenheit.

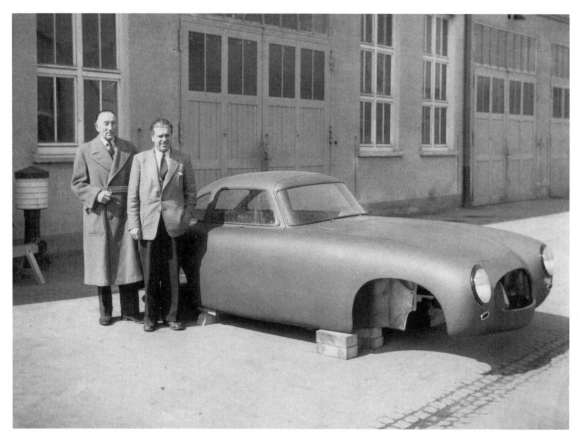

Uhlenhaut (right), seen here with one of the earliest bodyshells which had short doors, was involved from the start.

tension, not in bending) are the strongest of geometrical patterns in a single plane and are the basis for the strongest and lightest of structures when used as elements for building an extended three-dimensional framework.

The new racing chassis had deep side members joined by transverse triangulated beams in front of and behind the cockpit, and what looked like two skeletal pyramid structures at front and back, to carry the engine, transmission and suspension. The wheelbase had come down from the 120in (305cm) of the saloon and 114in (290cm) of the 300S to just 94½in (240cm), with the front track widened by a couple of inches and the rear left virtually unchanged.

At the front, the suspension was almost exactly identical to that of the saloon, except for a modest degree of lightening. It was independent, of course, with upper and lower wishbones of unequal length which were controlled by coil springs and telescopic dampers. In a familiar Mercedes refinement of the simple double wishbone layout, the inner wishbone pivots were not mounted rigidly to the chassis but were carried on a vertical post, which was itself mounted to the chassis, to allow a tiny amount of front-to-rear deflection (tightly limited by rubber stops). That was intended to absorb bump shocks and give slightly more compliance. There was also a conventional anti-roll bar.

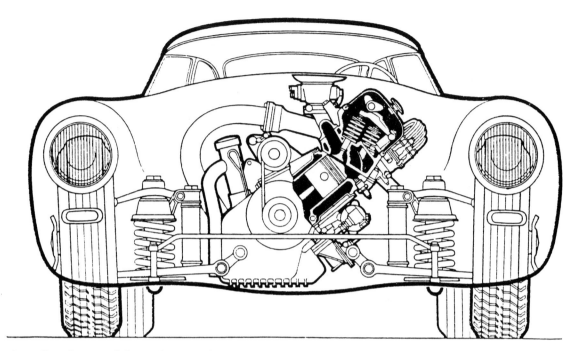

As well as the smooth lines, the major key to aerodynamic success lay in tilting the tall engine.

At the rear, Mercedes resisted the De Dion layout that they had used on their pre-war GP cars and instead adopted the swing axle set-up of the 300 saloon, this time with a bit more modification. Uhlenhaut in particular was an advocate of the swing axle, arguing that the De Dion cars had suffered axle tramp under maximum power where the swing axles did not, and that the swing axles were also more readily adjustable for under- or oversteer, by raising or lowering their pivot points. In this case, the half shafts (which pivoted at their inner ends on large horizontal trunnion bearings in the final drive unit casing) were controlled by coil springs and telescopic dampers. The latter were moved to sit behind the axles rather than in front (where they were on the saloon), and the supplementary torsion bars which could be switched into the saloon system by an electric solenoid (for additional stiffness with a full passenger load) were omitted from the much lighter sports racer.

The heavy saloon's brakes had frequently been criticized as one of its weaker points, and although the sports racer was obviously very much lighter, the brakes were uprated anyway, keeping the same diameter (inside similar diameter wheels) but being suitably wider and better cooled. The drums were of Al-fin construction, with a cast-iron inner ring chemically bonded directly into an alloy outer shell, which had radial fins for optimum cooling to improve both fade and wear resistance. The use of deeply dished wheels made room for the bigger brakes with enough airflow around them to work effectively. The Ferodo VG95 linings were also bonded rather than riveted to the shoes, and the hydraulic brake operation (with separate master cylinders for front and rear) was twin-leading-shoe at the front and single-leading-shoe at the back.

Rudi Uhlenhaut

If one man could be called the father of the whole SL family, that man would be Dr Ing Rudi Uhlenhaut who was Chief Development Engineer of Daimler-Benz when the racing 300SL was contrived, and later Research Director.

Uhlenhaut was in fact born in England, in Highgate in North London in July 1906. His mother was English and his father was a German banker whose work took him all around Europe. Rudi and his three brothers and sisters also lived briefly in Belgium before returning to a more permanent base in Germany in 1914. He spoke French, and of course German, but English had already become his second language and he remained an Anglophile all his life.

'I always knew I wanted to be an engineer', he once said, 'but when I was very young I had things mixed up a bit and I thought I wanted to be a locomotive engineer.' He soon found his true vocation though, and he graduated from Munich University in 1931, with a degree in mechanical engineering. Although this was in the worst of the Depression, he was employed almost at once by Daimler-Benz in Stuttgart.

He started his career working on production

Rudi Uhlenhaut shortly before his retirement, when he was Chief Passenger Car Development Engineer for Mercedes-Benz in Stuttgart.

cars, initially on carburation, and although he was not directly involved in Mercedes' return to GP racing in 1934, his experimental work certainly meant that the racing people knew he was there. Dr Fritz Nallinger had become the Engineering Director in 1934 after the untimely death of the brilliant Hans Nibel, and Uhlenhaut became his chief assistant. Their joint talents shaped much of Mercedes' future for many years, and led directly to the SLs.

Rudi officially joined the racing department late in 1936, after the Mercedes GP cars had suffered a season of unaccustomed mauling by Dr Porsche's Auto-Unions, and he became Technical Director. This was at a time when the racing department was funded by the government and absolutely everything was possible. At its height, the department had call on as many as 300 top engineers, designers and technicians, and Uhlenhaut was expected to get results. He did, with the awesome silver GP cars that won no less than nineteen of the twenty-eight GPs that were contested between 1937 and 1939.

At the core of Uhlenhaut's success was not just his design and engineering skills but the fact that he could also drive any car, the GP cars included, fast enough (and more importantly analytically enough) to have a unique first-hand perspective on what he was trying to achieve. He taught himself to do it with typical thoroughness; in effect, he simply took a car out and drove it faster and faster until he found his own limits and developed the techniques. In later years he was infinitely respected for his ability to lap the GP cars, or the racing sports cars, within a couple of per cent of the best times of any of his drivers – the likes of Fangio and Moss included – and to know with absolute precision what the car was doing and why. Right up to his retirement he was always on hand to take journalists out in the latest SL and show them what it could achieve.

The management perhaps worried about his frequent high-speed testing, but he never concerned them further by being tempted to race himself: 'The first time I drove at racing speeds I was 30, and that's a bit late to start. Yes, and then it would have been a waste of an engineer. We need engineers as well as drivers you know. That's the same reason why I never went to my limit, I don't think. I always tried to be on the safe side . . .'

More than anything, he completely reshaped traditional thinking on chassis and suspension behaviour, and it was his philosophical shift from ultra-stiff to suspension to stiff chassis and relatively soft springing that was one of the keys to the Mercedes' pre-war success – and of course continued after the war into the SLs and others.

During the war, Rudi worked on developing cold-climate military vehicles, and then on aero engines where he gained considerable experience of fuel-injection technology. After the war, the British military caretakers recognized his skills and with his faultless English he was an obvious choice to play a major part in the rebuilding programme. By 1948, with Daimler-Benz back into production, Uhlenhaut was in charge of the experimental department, and that was how he came to be in a position to inspire the SL as a return-to-racing project in the early 1950s.

Subsequently, he masterminded the mid-1950s return to GP racing with the totally dominant W196s, and the brief return to sports-car racing with the related 300SLRs. And, of course, he was involved in every SL programme right up to the most recent, in all except the last from planning stage all the way through to his famous demonstration drives at launch time.

After his retirement Rudi Uhlenhaut kept up the active life, travelling, sailing and skiing amongst other diversions. He died in May 1989, aged 82. He was still universally respected as one of the finest drivers never to race a GP car, as a man whose warmth and humour made the Mercedes racing teams far more relaxed and happy places than the awesome reputation for efficiency at any price might suggest, and most of all as one of the greatest automobile and racing engineers of them all.

A SMOOTH NEW SUIT

Since those days in the early 1930s when Mercedes had last been directly involved in sports car racing, one thing above all had changed: brute force had started to give way to science, and nowhere more so than in body design. It was no longer enough just to pile on the power; aerodynamics were now more and more the key to speed. Le Mans, with its unique 3.7-mile (5.6km) Mulsanne Straight where every car was expected to run flat out for a long period, was the ultimate test of that, as the victory of Jaguar's C-Type in 1951 would clearly have demonstrated to Mercedes' small band of observers had they not already known the fact.

The 3.4-litre C-Type with around 200bhp was in effect a slightly lighter, slightly more powerful version of the recently introduced production Jaguar sports car, the XK120, but with spaceframe underpinnings. Rebodied in a shell designed by Jaguar aerodynamics expert Malcolm Sayer, it made the absolute most of what power it had. It was designed specifically for Le Mans and the Mulsanne, and although it was by no means the most powerful car in the race that year, it was certainly the fastest. It recorded almost 144mph (232kph) on the long straight and one of the three cars entered finally won by over 60 miles (96km). That was in spite of the winning drivers, Peter Walker and Peter Whitehead, having to ease right back for much of the race, conscious of the fact that early mechanical problems had eliminated the other two team cars. They still covered a record 2,244 miles (3,611km), and before its retirement Moss's Jaguar set a new lap record at an average speed over 105mph (169kph) which showed Mercedes what they had to achieve.

The Jaguar was the first British winner since that Bentley swansong in 1931 at the expense of the lone works Mercedes, and that fact probably was not lost on the men from Stuttgart who could see the effect on Jaguar sales. After all, racing was only a means to an end; they had to get back into the production sports car market soon . . .

First though, their new racer was going to be even more aerodynamic than the Jaguar. It would have to be, because it was giving away almost half a litre and at least 25bhp, but Mercedes were aiming for an even higher top speed – 150mph (241kph) was the target. It would use all the tricks of smoothness that Mercedes had learned before the war with the GP racers and during it with involvement in military aircraft, plus the inclined engine and virtually no external trim. It would also be a coupé rather than an open car, which would give a major advantage – but also a major problem.

A FAMOUS SOLUTION

The problem was about combining the coupé bodywork with the very deep sided spaceframe chassis while still leaving a way for the driver to get in and out.

It was not just a practical problem as the rules were quite clear on what was required: Appendix C of the FIA's International Sporting Code specified that a sports car should have at least one 'door' capable of carrying a template of 16 × 8in (just under 40 × 20cm) and giving direct access to the seats. In the Mercedes, the side members of the spaceframe came up virtually to the seated driver's shoulder height, so there was no way of cutting the door into the flank in the conventional way. Also the roof line was so low that a simple opening side window would have been too small for anyone except a midget or a contortionist, so Mercedes had to innovate. Their solution, which eventually carried over on to the production derivative of the car, guaranteed the model eternal fame.

It was the 'gullwing' door, in which not only the side windows but also most of the roof were hinged from near the car's centre-line, to lift vertically – and when both were open it gave the car the look of a bird in flight. It was a practical and elegant way round the problem, which only later gave rise to doubts about how the driver would get out should the car happen to be inverted . . .

The first completed car, its styling largely the work of Karl Wilfert at Daimler-Benz's body design office in Sindelfingen, certainly looked the part. Before long, the doors would be extended a little way down into the flank, but as launched they stopped at the bottom edge of the side windows. The one-piece shell, formed in very thin aluminium sheet, was absolutely smooth, with no protruding external handles, no mirrors, no bumpers and the only trim being two large three-pointed stars in the generous radiator opening and on the opening boot panel. Even early plans to put a small step into the flank (to ease access over the deep sides) were soon dropped in favour of smoothness.

The roof line was not a full fast-back but more like a fixed hard top, with exceptionally slim pillars for fine all-round visibility, and the 'greenhouse' was markedly narrower than the lower body. The car was just over 49in (124cm) high, 70in (178cm) wide and 166in (422cm) long, on that 94½in (240cm) wheelbase; its frontal area was a little under 19½ sq ft (1.8 sq m) and the drag coefficient was said to be as low as 0.25Cd, which was a remarkable achievement. Apart from the grille, the car did not look unlike one of Porsche's early 356 lightweight coupés – which, perhaps not coincidentally, had marked Porsche's first ever entry at Le Mans, while the Mercedes observers were there in 1951.

SUPER-LIGHTWEIGHT SPORTSTER

Not only was it admirably slippery, it was also acceptably light. In spite of being really

Not a team driver, but comfortable in the well-trimmed cabin of an early 'short-door' coupé, with fully detachable steering wheel for ease of entry and exit.

rather luxuriously trimmed inside by racing car standards, with properly upholstered seats and even near-production-car standards of heating and ventilating equipment (Mercedes believed long-distance driver comfort was worth the weight penalty), it scaled only around 1,930lb (875 kg) without fuel and oil. Almost 600lb (272kg) of that was in the hefty 300 engine, but the outstandingly effective spaceframe complete with mounts for the alloy-panelled body contributed only some 110lb (50kg). For comparison

the 300 saloon weighed approximately 3,720lb (1,687kg) and even the more compact 300S was a 3,560lb (1,615kg) heavyweight.

The engine size, the new purpose and the remarkable weight saving were all acknowledged in the designation the factory gave the new car when it was revealed in public; they called it the 300SL, for *Super-Licht*, or super-lightweight.

The next step was to test it and, once that hurdle had been negotiated, to go racing and start winning . . .

3 Back to the Front: Testing and Racing the 300SL

The 300SL coupé was ready for its first test towards the end of 1951, barely six months after the racing department's exploratory outing to Le Mans. Appropriately enough, Chief Development Engineer Rudi Uhlenhaut was the first man to drive it, and none of the drivers who expected to race the car in the near future would have been offended by that. The leader of the SL design team was universally respected as one of those very rare individuals who was every bit as capable as a test driver as he was as an engineer, even in the GP cars; and when he tested the new coupé, he knew exactly what he was looking for.

Neubauer was in charge of the planning, and all the old thoroughness showed; he was, after all, the man who had often said

What else could it have been nicknamed? One of the first of the 'long-door' coupés, showing the brilliant solution to a difficult problem, and a complete lack of extraneous trim.

that the most important part of a racing victory lies in the preparation. In the early days of testing, the SL appeared at the Hockenheim circuit and on a convenient stretch of autobahn outside Stuttgart. When the car was tested on the autobahn the team erected an elaborate canvas garage – both for comfort and for security from prying eyes.

With few major modifications since it had first turned a wheel, the car, whose existence had been speculated on for some months, was first shown to the press in March 1952. It bore the 'registration' 300SL, and was received with predictable enthusiasm; many motoring commentators were already clearly anticipating great things from one of motor sport's most famous names.

Mercedes initially built four examples of the new SL, the earliest visible changes being the early loss of the step in the side below the doors, and a switch from the bolt-on all-steel wheels of the original to the Rudge-Whitworth centre-lock type, with steel centres and alloy rims. That had always been planned, but it appears that the car itself was ready before the new wheels and hubs.

THE RETURN TO THE CIRCUITS

Three cars were entered for the 300SL's racing début, on 4 May 1952, and they were thrown in at the deep end. The occasion was the Silver Jubilee of one of the world's most gruelling road races, the Mille Miglia, and the field that was due to set off from Brescia via Venice, Rimini, Pescara, Rome, Siena, Florence, Bologna, Modena, Parma and eventually back to Brescia some 980 miles (1,577km) later, ran to an astonishing 501 cars. Admittedly, the vast majority of them were entered in the plethora of small and specialized classes which were traditionally designed to give every conceivable breed of Italian car from the Topolino upwards a

The racer revealed; the deep-sided spaceframe and carburated engine of the definitive racing coupé.

chance to participate, but the 300SLs were there only to challenge for outright victory. With the serious end of the race becoming more serious than ever by 1952, Mercedes had set themselves a very hard task indeed.

They approached it with typical thoroughness. For some two months before the event the drivers and race engineers lived in Italy and did everything possible to learn the route and its secrets. Mercedes probably spent far more on their reconnaissance than most teams could even dream of spending on the whole race – reportedly including as much as £2,000 on petrol alone. The SLs were ferried from Stuttgart to Italy by road, accompanied by an impressive back-up team. *Motor Sport* magazine later commented that '. . . as the three silver cars drove down through Switzerland they created the impression that Mercedes-Benz were re-entering racing very near the point where they left off in 1939'.

The legendary organization faltered briefly though, when the 300SL's already famous gullwing doors (which at this stage still only extended down to window level) almost caused the car to be excluded from its first race. The scrutineers initially objected to them and took several hours to relent before they would let the SLs run.

Nor, in Italy of all places, could Mercedes expect a great deal of local encouragement for their racing return. In the great pre-war GP days, it was the German teams which had ended Italy's domination of the sport, and after the war the Italians had again become the people to beat.

In the eighteen epic races since 1927, the Mille Miglia had been to all intents and purposes an Italian benefit. The now defunct marque OM had won the first running, and of the rest, Alfa Romeo had won eleven and newcomers Ferrari had taken the last four in a row. Germany had been the interlopers in the other two races. A works BMW driven by von Hanstein and Baumer won in 1940 (when the race was run over nine laps of a shorter, 103-mile (166km) circuit and officially known as the 'Brescia GP', for political reasons), and Mercedes themselves had been the only other non-Italian winners back in 1931. Coincidentally, the streamlined BMW's which had dominated the 1940 event are widely regarded as having contributed quite significantly to the shape and the mechanical layout of the first XK Jaguars which appeared after the war, and whose racing cousins Mercedes would soon have to beat.

The drivers of the new generation of Silver Arrows, twenty years on from Mercedes' last Mille Miglia, were to be the Le Mans scouts, Karl Kling and Hermann Lang, plus the veteran Rudi Caracciola, now fifty-one but the man who had won the 1931 race in Mercedes' last sports car incarnation. In 1952 he was still the only non-Italian ever to have won it.

The three lead drivers were to be partnered, respectively by Hans Klenk, Erwin Gruppe and one Herr Kurrle. They would face a single works Jaguar C-Type driven by Stirling Moss (and testing new Dunlop disc brakes), no less than twenty-six Ferraris including a variety of works entries, and a number of very quick Alfas and Lancias, several of them with an outside chance of outright victory.

One-third of the Mercedes effort was very short lived. Shortly after the wet start in Brescia, Lang crashed into a roadside marker post and was out of the race, leaving just Kling and Caracciola to chase a Mercedes victory. Kling moved into second place behind Giovanni Bracco in the new Ferrari 250S – the first in the classic 250 line, and driven by 1951's second-placed driver. On the long fast run down the Adriatic coast from Rimini to Pescara, the initial promise of the surprisingly rapid Lancia coupés faded and the race settled into a head-to-head battle between the Ferraris and the Mercedes, briefly joined by Moss until he damaged the C-Type in a minor accident and fell back.

LEADING INTO ROME

Heading towards Pescara, Bracco's tyres were worn through to the canvas and Kling managed to haul him in, pass him and build around an eight-minute lead. Bracco's problems were made worse by the Ferrari crew in Pescara not having the correct front tyres for his car and being obliged to send him on to the next stop. That was right across the width of Italy, in Rome, which was always thought of as the start of the homeward run. It was also an old Mille Miglia adage that he who led in Rome would not win the race, and this year it was Kling and the 300SL who led into Rome . . .

By then Ferrari team leader Piero Taruffi in a 340S was second and Bracco had somehow managed to claw his way back from fifth to third. Castellotti's Ferrari, which had briefly held second, had crashed, Caracciola in the second surviving Mercedes was seventh into Rome, slowed by plug troubles, and some would also say because he was leaving it very late to make his charge.

By Florence the race was between Kling and the amazing Bracco. Taruffi had gone out with transmission failure and the rest were well adrift. Bracco, a textile executive from Biella, had won his class in the previous year's race driving a Lancia, and had finished second overall behind Villoresi's Ferrari. He was already building a reputation as a driver teetering on the borderline between genius and madness. After Florence the race headed almost due north to Bologna, over the Appenine mountains, through the 2,960ft (902m) high Futa Pass and over the even more daunting 3,170ft (966m) Raticosa Pass, all wreathed in clouds and with terrifying, unprotected drops flanking the roads. Bracco chain-smoked in the car and his co-driver passed him sips of brandy from a hip-flask; yet somehow, by Bologna he had forced his way past Kling and into the lead.

He stayed there all the way to Brescia, and one of the most remarkable victories in the history of motor racing. Kling was second, four and a half minutes adrift, while Caracciola held on to fourth, another thirty-four minutes down. But for Bracco's inspired madness, the 300SL would undoubtedly have been celebrating its début with victory . . .

THE FIRST SUCCESS

In fact the first win followed very soon after; not anything so prestigious as snatching the Mille Miglia would have been, but a win nonetheless. It was in the sports car race supporting the Swiss GP in Berne, and Mercedes had entered the same three drivers – Kling, Lang and Caracciola, plus an extra car for Fritz Riess. The fourth car was the first example of the 300SL with the deeper doors, which now extended down a few inches into the flanks. They were Mercedes' reaction to the problems in Mille Miglia scrutineering, and had been designed in preparation for Le Mans, where Neubauer meant to take no chances with the whims of the notoriously xenophobic French officials . . .

Of the four cars at Berne, one was painted red, one blue, one green and one silver, apparently in deference to Switzerland being a neutral country. What little opposition they had was eliminated right at the start, when the sole Ferrari, which was a works car and had been on pole position, broke its transmission on the starting line.

Thereafter, the race was effectively a 300SL demonstration, with Kling, Lang and Riess cruising around to take the first three places. Caracciola was fourth until he spoiled the clean sweep with a big accident on the thirteenth lap when his brakes locked (a problem also seen on Kling's car in the Mille Miglia), and he spun off and hit a tree. His leg was badly broken (not for the first time in his life) and he spent most of the rest of 1952 in traction. That was the end of the career of one of the greatest of all Mercedes' drivers. It slightly tempered the start of the career of one of their greatest cars.

THE MAJOR PRIZE

Still, Mercedes had four cars ready for the next race and this was the big one, Le Mans, in mid-June 1952.

This was what everything had been geared to for the year since Neubauer, Kling and Lang had made their recce. Three new cars were built for the race, with the deeper doors now standard wear. Again, preparation was everything.

The team was on full song right from the start of practice, where in addition to the three silver team cars they had a spare car finished in red and another test-bed car in silver, this one with an experimental air brake mounted on pylons to sit about 12in (30cm) above the roof. It was operated by a lever in the cockpit, which enabled the driver to move it into a vertical position for braking from very high speeds, and automatically returned it to the horizontal when the speed fell below 100mph (161kph), from where the normal, finned drum brakes did the rest.

The air brake was tried at Le Mans because the aerodynamics of the body were proving so effective that the car had very little aerodynamic braking of its own. This meant the engine and brakes were taking even more of the strain than they normally would from maximum speed. It was an idea which the team would use to great effect in a slightly different form a year or two hence, but for the moment, although the movable 'wing' did its job in terms of braking, the pillars that supported it were not quite strong enough to risk for twenty-four difficult hours. What it did suggest, though, was that the big Al-fin drums were still not much better than marginal for the 300SL, and disc brakes such as Jaguar were pioneering would obviously have to appear

sooner or later. (Surprisingly perhaps, it was later. The racers never did use them and nor did the production coupé; Mercedes did not finally go 'modern' until the production 300SL Roadster appeared, in 1957.)

During Le Mans practice the drivers mostly circulated in the spare and experimental cars, while the three first-string cars underwent final preparation for the race. Come the day, their main opposition would obviously come from among the seven Ferraris entered (led by Ascari in a works 250S similar to the one with which Bracco had won the Mille Miglia) and the works Jaguars. In the event, it was not so much the Mercedes that triumphed as the opposition that crumbled – but either way the result was the same.

The Mercedes were driven by the Mille Miglia second place pairing of Kling and Klenk (the second crew member at Le Mans actually doing fair shares of the driving, as opposed to the Mille Miglia where they were largely navigators and in the car throughout), by Lang and Riess, and Theo Helfrich with Norbert Niedermayer.

RUNNING TO SCHEDULE

The team had not gone for outright speed so much as for reliability, all orchestrated by Neubauer's legendary planning. Their engines were in a milder than usual state of tune, by maybe 5bhp, and in the end the experiments on the experimental car remained just that. In the race they intended to run to their own schedule and let the opposition do what it might. On the dashboard of each of the SLs would be a clock and a written list of times for refuelling and other pit calls.

Air outlets were let into the roof lines behind the gullwing doors to make the comfortably ventilated cockpits with their tartan cloth seats and removable steering wheels even more comfortable in the expected heat; Neubauer even made it easier for his drivers to identify their pit at speed (and rubbed home the publicity) by having a large Mercedes star in place over the garages.

When the race started, Ascari in the 3-litre V12 Ferrari (with maybe 60bhp more than the Mercedes) tore off into the lead and immediately set a new lap record, at over 107mph (172kph). Within a couple of laps, though, he was in trouble with a slipping clutch and within three hours it had failed completely and the fastest Ferrari was out of the race.

The Jaguar challenge had already gone and ironically, the C-Types' failure was almost certainly prompted by the speed of the 300SLs in the Mille Miglia. Moss had declared after that race that the Jaguars could not hope to beat the Mercedes at Le Mans without more straight-line speed; accordingly, the C-Type's body had been slightly revised, with a longer nose and tail

for better aerodynamics, but as it transpired this was at the expense of creating overheating problems. The problems showed up in practice and Jaguar hastily uprated the radiators, but not by enough, and within an hour all three works C-Types were out of Le Mans. The irony was that the 300SLs had not been nearly as quick as Moss and Jaguar had anticipated, and only Ascari's Ferrari had actually been quicker than the C-Types.

For a while, other Ferraris were also quicker than the Mercedes. A 340 coupé entered by the North American Racing Team led briefly but it would be the only Ferrari to finish, and that would be a long way back in fifth place. Of the others, the second Ferrari works car (a 225 Berlinetta) was just about on the pace until it was put out by electrical failure. Chinetti's 340 was disqualified for refuelling one lap early (which must have amused Neubauer) and the rest broke – all as Mercedes had anticipated.

Just a year after he had been in the scouting party, Kling shared a car at Le Mans with Klenk which proved to be the fastest of the three entries, but they retired when the dynamo failed . . .

. . . leaving Lang and Riess to inherit a well-judged if slightly fortunate win . . .

*. . . ahead of the Helfrich and Niedermayer car which finished second and just
over a lap behind.*

Some of the other opposition may have surprised them slightly. For quite a while the race was led by a small but indecently quick 2.3-litre twin-cam six-cylinder Gordini, until it ran out of brakes. That left the lead to another French car, a 4½-litre Talbot-Lago driven by Pierre Levegh and René Marchand; or more accurately by Levegh, who inherited the lead having driven the whole race thus far solo; and having seen how he was pulling away from the pursuing Mercedes he had resolved to go it alone – something that the rules were soon changed to prohibit.

Two-thirds of the way through the race, although his tiredness was making his driving rather untidy in places, Levegh had a four-lap lead, and right through Sunday there seemed no chance that anyone, Mercedes included, would catch him. Then with barely an hour to go his exhaustion finally settled the matter; he selected a wrong gear, broke the engine and his race was over – heroically but conclusively.

In 1955, Levegh, largely because of the way he had impressed the team with his 1952 efforts, would be in the Mercedes team at Le Mans. Then he would be driving one of the sensational GP-based 300SLR racing sports cars, but that drive would result in even greater tragedy.

Meanwhile, in the 1952 race, the 300SLs were running at their own pace; or at least two of them were, because the Kling/Klenk car was put out of the race by dynamo failure – shades of the Caracciola failure back in 1930. Before it failed it had been the quickest of the 300SLs, lapping in 4m 46s, or at an average of 105.5mph (169.8kph) which was marginally quicker than Moss's lap record of 1951 but not quite as quick as Ascari's new mark. In the race the quickest Mercedes was recording some 6,100rpm in top gear on the Mulsanne Straight, equivalent to about 152mph (245kph).

But for Levegh's missed gear, it would not have been enough, of course, but as the

Talbot went out, the Lang and Riess 300SL inherited the lead (Neubauer would undoubtedly say that this was according to plan) and reeled off the remaining hour to win. It was followed home by the little-known third-string pairing of Helfrich and Niedermayer in the remaining car. The winner had covered 2,320 miles (3,734km) at an average of 96.7mph (155.6kph) and the runner up was just under 9 miles (14.5km), or a whisker over one lap, adrift.

Had you been there, you could hardly have said the Mercedes were dominant, but the record book said 'Mercedes 1-2' and that was what counted in the end . . .

ROADSTERS FOR THE 'RING

The next time the mighty 300SLs appeared, for the sports car race supporting the German GP at Nurburgring in August, the team would rely on a new, open variant of the car. Three of these roadsters were devised by the relatively simple expedient of chopping the tops off the existing coupés (including two of the Le Mans cars) and a fourth was built from scratch, on an 8in (20cm) shorter wheelbase and with other minor body changes. The interior trim was lightened somewhat because there was no longer any need for additional air conditioning, the bottoms of the doors were left as simple lift-out panels, and even the instrumentation was reduced to a bare minimum. The thinking behind all this was that on a slower and more difficult circuit like the tortuous Nurburgring, aerodynamics would be less important than at Le Mans, and lightness and visibility would be more important.

The team appeared with no less than six cars in practice at the Nurburgring, the four new roadsters and two of the 'conventional' coupés. They were experimenting again, too; one of each variant (coupé and roadster) was tried with supercharging (using Roots-type blowers mounted on the right of the engine, gear driven and with heavily ribbed casings), but they were not raced because they gave problems with overheating during the practice outings.

The team did not actually need the extra power; the opposition was again relatively modest, led by a quasi-works 340 Ferrari from the Marzotto team, and a single works 2.3 Gordini such as the one which had been so surprising at Le Mans. The Ferrari simply was not quick enough and the Gordini broke its gearbox, which left the Mercedes to complete another demonstration run. Again, it was not quite faultless, as Kling lost the lead through an oil leak which was lubricating his rear tyres. The only real effect of that, though, was to juggle the 300SLs' 1–2–3–4 finishing order so that Kling was behind Lang and ahead of Riess and Helfrich. The winning car was the same one that had won at Le Mans, but now, of course, *sans* roof . . .

THE TOUGHEST TEST OF ALL

To round off the season, Mercedes set themselves what was probably the toughest test of all, in the third running of the Carrera Panamericana. This Mexican Road Race involved some 2,000 miles (3,219km) and five days of the highest speed racing, on public roads and in often desperately hard conditions, from the heat and dust of the day into the chill of the night. The course ran from sea level at Tehuantepec to almost 10,500ft (3,200m) in the mountains, and the fastest of the eight legs could mean average speeds of close to 140mph (225kph) for literally hundreds of miles at a stretch, with the inevitable strains on both the cars and their drivers.

Gunther Molter, assistant to Neubauer for the race and delegated as press agent, wrote in *Auto* magazine soon after the event:

Within two years this race had achieved a reputation second to neither the Mille Miglia nor Le Mans. It was a race demanding 100 per cent participation, a race admirably suited to the ancient racing tradition of Daimler-Benz. At that time we didn't know too much about the *Carrera*. We were only able to piece together a rough picture of the course and conditions from brief conversations at Indianapolis with Tony Bettenhausen and other former participants. Then one day we were ready to start . . .

Of course, there was a great deal more to Mercedes' preparation than that, as Molter's excellent post-race account went on to reveal: the following description is largely based on his report . . .

Although the race was not until mid-November, the two coupés and two roadsters (one of the latter a back-up car, and in fact the one that had won both Le Mans and the Nurburgring race) were shipped from Hamburg in September, headed for Veracruz. They were followed by the team personnel and drivers, who flew out late in October with ample time to do their usual thorough reconnaissance.

The drivers were to be the familiar pairing of Kling and Klenk, and Lang and Gruppe in the two coupés, plus American recruit John Fitch in the roadster with Eugen Geiger.

Fitch was Mercedes' first American driver and he was a fine choice. His racing career would last barely ten years, but he became one of the best road racers ever to come out of America. He had spent a couple of months in Germany at the end of World War II, interned after being shot down while he was a Mustang fighter pilot. He started racing in 1949, bitten by the sports car bug like so many other young Americans who had spent time in Europe during the War. By 1951 he had won an SCCA championship and had driven for Briggs Cunningham at Le Mans – running as high as second place for some time. He had already raced in the Carrera too, in 1951 in a 6-litre Chrysler Saratoga; in fact he had been leading the race when the engine failed after some 350 miles (563km).

In 1952 he had been back at Le Mans for Cunningham and had led that race too, albeit very briefly, from the start. Mechanical problems dropped him to last but he fought his way back to third before going out with engine failure.

Mercedes, though, had already noticed his efforts, and they had the chance to see him again at the Nurburgring race, where he finished fourth (behind the three 300SLs) in a Porsche. Neubauer gave him a test drive in a 300SL at the Nurburgring and Fitch (perhaps to Neubauer's surprise) was impressed. He was a natural choice for Mercedes for the 1952 Carrera, and in 1955 he would be back as a fully fledged sports car team member with one of the second generation 300s.

PREPARING TO WIN

Back to the 1952 Carrera, the team set up headquarters in Mexico City with around thirty-five personnel and two transporters full of equipment. On 25 October the drivers started practising on the southern legs of the course. Eventually, each driver had driven each leg of the course in practice, and in fact Lang set what would have been a new record for the first leg (from Tuxtla to Oaxaca) while the road was still open to ordinary traffic.

The drivers and co-drivers made endless notes both on potential hazards and on places where they could expect to gain time; the team worked out what the demands of the course implied in terms of roadside servicing and especially of tyre wear. Continental did not have time to develop a special tyre (as the decision to race in Mexico had apparently been taken quite late) but they supplied around 300 covers for the sort of fast, curving

roads that they anticipated. Once he had inspected the course, Neubauer arranged for nine roadside tyre depots to be set up, and he marked their approach with the familiar three-pointed star. Bosch, as normal, supplied the electrical equipment but Mercedes chose to use American-manufactured Valvoline oil.

In theory the organizing club was to supply the 80-octane Avgas in drums, but having tested with it and found it lacking, Mercedes arranged for a supply that was actually as good as the regulations allowed.

The team arrived at the Tuxtla Guttierez starting point with a couple of days in hand for final preparations, the race cars having been driven to the start.

The race had hardly started when Lang was in trouble. At somewhere near 125mph (201kph) he hit a dog, escaping without any mechanical damage (which was more than could be said for the dog) but bending the front bodywork badly enough to knock a few mph off the top speed. Problems with the local wildlife continued when the Kling/Klenk car hit a buzzard at almost 140mph (225kph) the bird smashing right through the windscreen and into Klenk's face – and he had removed his crash helmet during a tyre change at Tehuantepec. The impact left him bloody and briefly unconscious, obliging Kling to stop and wait for him to recover; but the pair continued.

Fitch, the tall American, in the roadster, was fortunate not to hit anything at all; the small additional windshield he had had mounted in front of his face on tall stalks was reasonable protection from the buffeting wind, but probably even less use against a heavy bird than the coupé's laminated windscreen had proved to be.

AN UNACCUSTOMED HICCUP

The first leg gave the cars other problems too, with tyres. Looking at the many curves

*The team had its share of giants; Neubauer congratulating John Fitch in one of
the open 300SLs – with additional windscreen for the lanky American.*

in the road, the team had chosen a 'Nurburgring-type' tyre, with a strong but heavy tread. The long straight sections in fact made these tyres overheat very badly and all three cars had to change tyres three times during the first leg. As Molter admitted, 'Since this had not been anticipated, Kling lost 12m 36s and our team entered Oaxaca in third, seventh and eighth positions. It was hard maintaining our composure . . .'

Neubauer's plan, however, not unlike that at Le Mans, was to keep to a careful pace until the race reached Mexico City, and then go flat out to the finish – circumstances permitting.

As at Le Mans, the most obvious threat was Ascari in a works 340 Ferrari, which was far more powerful and potentially quicker than the Mercedes, but potentially more fragile – especially if its driver was racing without the sort of disciplined pacing worked out by Neubauer.

The Mercedes' servicing system was also second to none; Lang's dog-inflicted body-work damage (already hastily patched up at the roadside after the accident) was properly repaired in Mexico City and Kling's windscreen was replaced during the second night, after an enthusiastic Mexican politician, having heard of the buzzard incident on the radio, had offered his own private aeroplane to get a spare windscreen to distant Oaxaca.

After Mexico City (and once Ferrari driver Villoresi had been sidelined by rear axle trouble) the race developed into an epic battle between two familiar rivals, Kling for Mercedes and Bracco for Ferrari – the same pair who had had such a desperate struggle in the Mille Miglia. Kling started with the advantage but lost it with recurring tyre problems, leaving the famously uninhibited Bracco in the lead.

Between Durango and Parral the two raced on the absolute limits, but this time it was Kling who managed to claw his way ahead, by several minutes before Parral.

Fitch was still in the running but was about to be disqualified. Short of servicing time before his official start slot, he started the next stage with a steering problem, then reversed over the start line, back a short way along the course, to the Mercedes service depot. His intention had been to have the problem fixed and only then to worry about making up lost time. As he reversed, a mechanic came out to help him, technically outside the depot. That in itself was against the rules, but had it not been, driving in the wrong direction on the course most certainly was anyway. Many other teams lodged protests, and Neubauer – who must have been incensed by such a basic organizational error – had no basis to argue. Fitch was disqualified at Chihuahua, but on Neubauer's request he was allowed to drive the rest of the route as a non-combatant.

Lang, too, had problems on the penultimate stage when his driver's door was blown away, but he continued without it.

Unofficially, Fitch was the fastest driver of all on the final leg, but Kling was the one who took the honours. As Bracco fell back, and finally out, with a rear axle failure, Kling averaged more than 132mph (212kph) over the last stretch – to round off the 300SL's brilliant season with perhaps the hardest won laurels of all.

A CHANGE OF DIRECTION

At the end of his *Auto* report, Gunther Molter wrote:

Our victory was a great event, especially since all three Mercedes-Benz cars reached the goal. The engines were still running smoothly and all of the cars went the 1,364 miles back to Mexico City under their own power. We returned to Germany after a wonderful race in a friendly country, *Hasta la vista, caballeros* . . . until 1953.

In fact the 300SLs never went back to Mexico, or to any other race. Having won all but the first of the five races they had entered in 1952, including the two most prestigious of all, Mercedes obviously felt no obligation to go out and repeat the feat in 1953.

Besides, they now had a new racing target in that they were at last planning a return to GP racing with the coming of the new formula in 1954.

So ended the short but glorious career of the racing 300SL; in a couple of years' time, the racing sports car would be back in the guise of the W196 GP-car-derived 300SLRs; but for their next step Mercedes had different plans for the 300SL, as an extremely desirable production sports car . . .

4 Into Production: The Gullwing Coupé

When Mercedes went into the 300SL racing programme, they did so with the intention of relaunching the marque's sporting image, and without doubt they *did* intend to build sports cars for the public as soon in the future as their rapidly recovering circumstances would allow; but the 300SL was not supposed to be it, not yet.

As much as for anything, Mercedes had used the 300SL racing programme as a relatively low-budget, toe-in-the-water exercise, designed to play themselves back into international motor sport. However, the long-term intention was always to re-enter the considerably higher-profile world of GP racing as soon as the formula changed.

Had they not won so convincingly throughout 1952, and had they not by then learned everything they thought they were going to learn in the short term, they might well have continued with the sports car programme for 1953; in fact that was probably the original intention. It was also said to be part of the original intention that Mercedes would build a 'production' run of 300SLs – this did not mean the road car that was soon to appear, but rather a small number of cars to expand the racing effort to selected private owners. Given the production sourcing of most of the car's major components, that could have been a comparatively easy move, perhaps even a profitable one.

A silver arrow for the road. During translation into a production car, the 300SL had kept its sleek profile little changed, but added many practical and styling touches.

NOTHING MORE TO PROVE?

Having won four of the five races they had contested, though, and finished second in the other, they had little left to prove. What is more, they had enjoyed an exceptional amount of sparkling publicity for really quite a modest effort. When they won, they won well, but it has to be said that the opposition was rarely better than moderate; and for all the organization, luck smiled on them too (or at least frowned on others) to turn Neubauer's hunches into results. In none of the big three races – the Mille Miglia, Le Mans and the Carrera Panamericana – were the Silver Arrows the fastest cars, but in two of them they won as others

300SL COUPÉ, 1954–57

Body type	: two-door, two-seater 'gullwing' coupé
Chassis	: multi-tubular spaceframe
Engine type	: in-line six-cylinder
Capacity	: 2,996cc
Bore	: 85.0mm
Stroke	: 88.0mm
Compression ratio	: 8.5:1
Cylinders	: cast-iron block, seven main bearings
Cylinder head	: alloy, with two valves per cylinder operated by single, chain-driven, overhead camshaft
Fuel system	: Bosch direct mechanical injection
Maximum power	: 240bhp at 6,100rpm
Maximum torque	: 217lb ft at 4,800rpm
Bhp per litre	: 80.1
Gearbox type	: four-speed manual
Gear ratios	: Fourth: 1.00 Second: 1.97
	Third: 1.38 First: 3.38
	Reverse: 3.38
Final drive ratio	: options included 4.11, 3.89, 3.64, 3.42, 3.25:1
Clutch	: single dry-plate
Front suspension	: unequal-length double wishbones, coil springs, telescopic dampers, anti-roll bar
Rear suspension	: high-pivot swing axles, coil springs, telescopic dampers
Brakes	: Al-fin steel/alloy composite drums all round; hydraulic with vacuum assistance
Steering	: recirculating ball
Wheels and tyres	: alloy/steel composite wheels; 6.70 × 15in cross-ply tyres (radials optional)
Overall length	: 175.0in (444.5cm)
Overall width	: 70.0in (177.8cm)
Overall height	: 51.0in (129.5cm)
Wheelbase	: 94.6in (240.3cm)
Track	: 54.6in (138.7cm) front; 56.5in (143.5cm) rear
Ground clearance	: 5.2in (13.2cm)
Fuel tank capacity	: 28gal (127 litres)
Unladen weight	: 2,720lb (1,234kg)
Power to weight ratio	: 197.6bhp/ton

PERFORMANCE

Maximum speed	: depending on gearing (*see* text)
0–60mph (0–97kph)	: 7.0sec
0–100mph (0–161kph)	: 16.2sec
Standing ¼ mile (0.4km)	: 15.4sec
Fuel consumption	: approx 17mpg (6km per litre)

[300SL Roadster, 1957–63, is mechanically as 300SL coupé except for the following principal differences: body with folding soft-top or removable hard-top; engine used 'sport' camshaft as standard and produced 250bhp at 6,200rpm; rear suspension was by low-pivot swing axle; from 1961, disc brakes were used all round; front track 55.1in (139.9cm), rear track 57.1in (145.0cm); unladen weight 3,050lb (1,384kg); maximum speed approx 130mph (209kph).]

broke, and in the third (the Mille Miglia) neither they nor anyone else had the answer to Bracco's mixture of inspired madness and mechanical good fortune.

Denis Jenkinson (a man who was to be involved famously with Mercedes' next sports racing car incarnation as Moss's winning co-driver in the 1955 Mille Miglia), writing in *Motor Sport* in April 1953, analysed the situation typically perceptively:

While others broke down, Mercedes-Benz did not, while others did not enter, Mercedes-Benz did, and while others said what they could do, Mercedes-Benz did what they set out to do. At the beginning of 1953 when everyone was musing on this season's sports car races a note arrived from Stuttgart to the effect that the 300SL cars would not be raced in 1953 as the last season had proved all they had set out to do, the race organization had been proved, the drivers had been well tested for future projects and Mercedes-Benz had proved that their cars were the finest in the world. As an afterthought it was mentioned that in addition to the above reasons for withdrawing from racing for 1953, the factory would be too busily engaged in preparing the team for the 1954 Grand Prix season. All this caused quite a bit of havoc one way and another. Ferrari and his men were hopping mad as they considered they had the best sports car, while everyone else pondered deeply on the final part of the Stuttgart statement. Ferrari challenged Mercedes-Benz to prove their sports car claim, but this was turned down with the polite statement that there had been ample opportunity during 1952 and anyway they were not interested in beating challengers, being more concerned with winning races . . .

DEVELOPMENT CONTINGENCIES

If Mercedes *had* decided to continue in 1953,

they had at least been doing enough work on the cars to close the apparent gap on those who felt cheated. Most of the effort had been directed towards finding more power, and the majority of that came from work on the M186 engine's breathing. Changing the downdraught Solex carburettors for down-draught Webers added 10bhp or more, to around 190bhp, and then more fundamental changes to the cylinder head, with very slightly bigger inlet valves and ports, took maximum power to just over 200bhp for the first time, and peak torque to a little over 200lb ft.

That was still not as much as the Italian and English opposition, but the Mercedes engines remained totally reliable, and there were chassis improvements to come too. The larger wheels and tyres which Neubauer had been asking for from the start (in 16in diameter rather than 15in) had been tried and, amazingly, further small gains were even found in the aerodynamics.

Mercedes also tried a different rear axle layout – the type that would appear in production in 1953 on the all-new 180 saloon, which was Mercedes' first unit construction model. This layout kept the 'high-pivot' swing axles (with their pivots parallel to the centre axis of the car and at the mid-height of the final-drive unit), but complemented them with fabricated lower trailing links.

The links were mounted on flexible rubber bushes to the chassis at their front ends and to the brake backplate at the wheel end. That maintained the effective length of the original swing axles while taking some of the braking and drive torque loads, allowing the axles themselves to be lighter and there-fore the sprung weight to be reduced. It was not, however, a complete solution to the roll oversteer problems associated with the high pivot, and a better palliative would not appear until the production launch of the smaller first generation SL, the 190SL, late in 1954, with the 'low-pivot' arrangement of the new 220 saloons.

It did not need to say much on the nose or tail to prove that the 300SL was something special.

During 1952, Uhlenhaut's men also started looking towards fuel injection as the key to more substantial power increases on the racing engine – this was at a time when petrol injection for cars was virtually unheard of. That was not because it was theoretically inferior – in fact it was far from it – but because until then several manufacturers, and Weber in particular, had developed multiple-choke carburettors to the point where they were virtually as good in performance as, yet substantially cheaper than, any early practicable injection system.

The Bosch direct injection as tried on the M186 engine took power output to some 208bhp with the original cylinder heads and as high as 214bhp with the slightly bigger valves. (Direct in this context means directly into the cylinders, diesel engine style, whereas virtually all the systems that we are familiar with today are indirect – that is, injecting upstream of the inlet valves, into the inlet tracts.) Had Mercedes

(Opposite) *The production car had the same low, wide stance and narrow cockpit, with just a bit more chrome around the nose.*

gone racing in 1953 they would undoubtedly have used the injection, but its first appearance was no longer to be reserved for the race track.

STEALING THE SHOW

At the 1954 New York Motor Sport Show Mercedes unveiled the 300SL as a fully-equipped and stunningly specified production model. It shared the limelight with a smaller and less extreme new production roadster, the 2-litre, 125bhp, four-cylinder 190SL (of which more later), but naturally it was the 300 that stole the show.

Had things been left to Mercedes alone, the production 300SL would not have happened when it did, and in fact it probably would not have happened at all in a form so close to the original racers. There was certainly a growing market for sports cars though, as the world regained prosperity after the war and people made the most of their new sense of freedom. Nowhere was the market bigger or faster growing than in America, where young men returning from

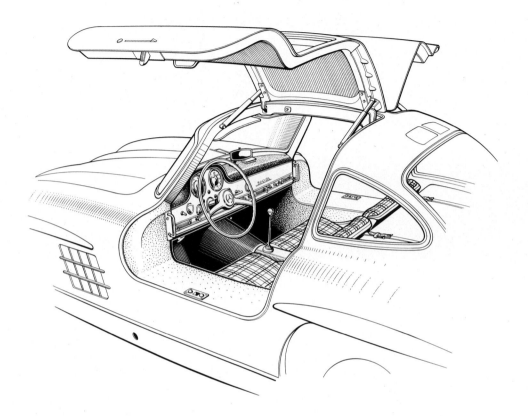

The door, sill and cockpit layout survived almost unchanged from race-track to road.

European tours of military duty had taken the European sports car ethic home with them and showed how a small engine and taut chassis could run rings round the typical American car, with its huge V8 but wallowingly soft gait.

America was even taking to European-style road racing as an alternative to their traditional oval-based events, and when Mercedes won the highly publicized Carrera Panamericana right on North America's doorstep they made absolutely certain that their 1952 racing efforts would not go unnoticed on that side of the Atlantic either.

They had a problem in so far as Mercedes sales had only resumed in the USA at the end of 1952, but the firm's reputation was such that the market had been strong right from the start. They just needed a little time

to add the sports car line as icing on the cake.

MAX HOFFMAN – A MAN WITH VISION

The final catalyst for the production 300SL came from America itself, from one Maximilian 'Max' Hoffman, who was the new Mercedes importer in New York and a sports car enthusiast through and through. He was an American of Austrian descent, and his Park Avenue dealership had almost single-handedly been responsible for re-opening the American market to European cars (and especially to European sports cars) soon after the war.

Max formed close ties with BMW and

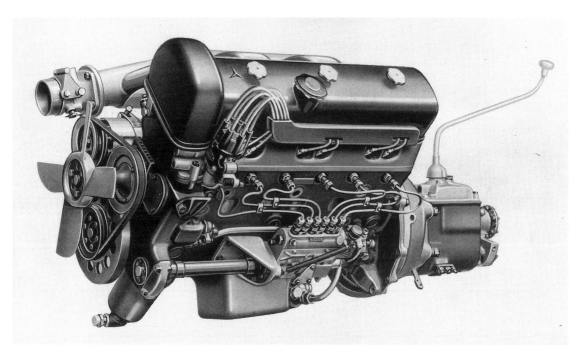

*The change to direct fuel injection for the production 300SL engine was a
pioneering move. This shot also shows just how far the engine was tilted.*

Volkswagen, and of course with Mercedes,
but his most important early contact was
with Porsche. He had met Dr Ferdinand
Porsche at the Paris Motor Show in October
1950 and arranged to import the first
Porsches into America; in 1952 he looked
after Dr Porsche's son, Ferry, on his second
post-war visit to the USA. This was when
Porsche were acting as consultants to Stude-
baker on the basis of introductions made by
Hoffman (and the Studebaker-Packard Cor-
poration would also become US distributors
for the production SLs); Hoffman would
devise the chopped-down Speedster version
of the Porsche 356, and it was even Max who
around 1952 urged Porsche to come up with
a proper badge. He sat with Ferry Porsche
in a New York restaurant while the latter
sketched a 'coat of arms' on the back of a
napkin, with the crest of the House of Wur-
temberg and the rampant horse of the coat of
arms of the city of Stuttgart, all surmounted

by the Porsche name. Within a year the
sketch had become the official Porsche badge.

Also by 1953, Porsche were beginning to
enter their first races in the USA, naturally
with the help of Hoffman; and that brought
an important Mercedes contact.

Porsche racing manager Baron Huschke
von Hanstein (the same one who had won
the 1940 Mille Miglia for BMW) recounts in
Porsche: Portrait of a Legend (Orbis, London; 1985; compiled by Ingo Seiff), how one
trip brought Hoffman together with Karl
Kling, the Mercedes works driver, and winner
of the 1952 Carrera in the 300SL racer. Porsche had 'borrowed' Kling from Mercedes, but
when the group arrived in New York by ship
from Hamburg on a Friday afternoon Kling
was detained by the immigration authorities
and, in spite of efforts from the German
Embassy, he spent the weekend in a cell on
Ellis Island – the notorious gateway to all
would-be American immigrants.

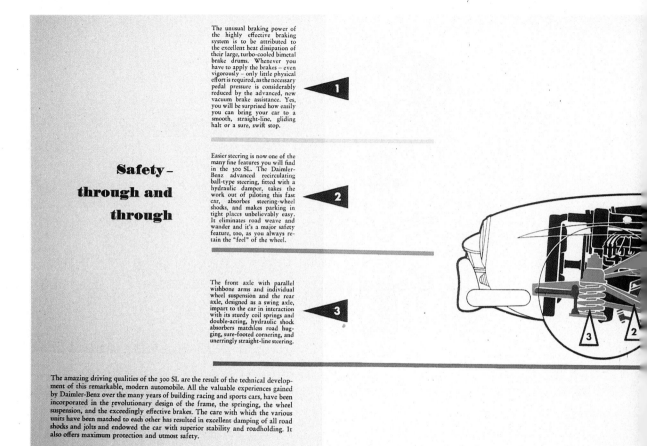

Safety – through and through

The unusual braking power of the highly effective braking system is to be attributed to the excellent heat dissipation of their large, turbo-cooled bimetal brake drums. Whenever you have to apply the brakes – even vigorously – only little physical effort is required, as the necessary pedal pressure is considerably reduced by the advanced, new vacuum brake assistance. Yes, you will be surprised how easily you can bring your car to a smooth, straight-line, gliding halt or a sure, swift stop.

Easier steering is now one of the many fine features you will find in the 300 SL. The Daimler-Benz advanced recirculating ball-type steering, fitted with a hydraulic damper, takes the work out of piloting this fast car, absorbes steering-wheel shocks, and makes parking in tight places unbelievably easy. It eliminates road weave and wander and it's a major safety feature, too, as you always retain the "feel" of the wheel.

The front axle with parallel wishbone arms and individual wheel suspension and the rear axle, designed as a swing axle, impart to the car in interaction with its sturdy coil springs and double-acting, hydraulic shock absorbers matchless road hugging, sure-footed cornering, and unerringly straight-line steering.

The amazing driving qualities of the 300 SL are the result of the technical development of this remarkable, modern automobile. All the valuable experiences gained by Daimler-Benz over the many years of building racing and sports cars, have been incorporated in the revolutionary design of the frame, the springing, the wheel suspension, and the exceedingly effective brakes. The care with which the various units have been matched to each other has resulted in excellent damping of all road shocks and jolts and endowed the car with superior stability and roadholding. It also offers maximum protection and utmost safety.

Racing technology for the road; the 300SL's complex spaceframe and all-independent suspension paid a lot less attention to cost than to strength and lightness.

Hoffman had arranged a party to introduce the Porsche people to the press on the Monday and Kling was meant to be the guest of honour, but come Monday he was still locked up, even though an American millionairess had offered to expedite his release by marrying him if necessary! She did not have to; Von Hanstein stood in at the party and Kling, without ever having been told why he had been detained in the first place, was released in the evening and joined the group to talk of Porsche and Mercedes, and of racing and sports cars in general, with Max and the others.

AN IRRESISTIBLE OFFER

So now, in 1953, Hoffman was convinced that there was a market for a production version of the car which had brought Mercedes back into the sporting limelight with such a bang, and when Mercedes did not immediately share his enthusiasm, he dangled the irresistible carrot of a firm order for 1,000 such cars, if Mercedes were willing to build them.

It was an offer they could hardly refuse, and come January 1954 the result was there

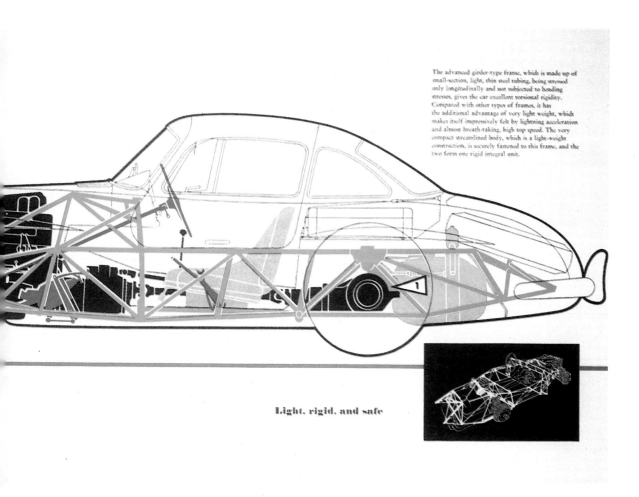

The advanced girder-type frame, which is made up of small-section, light, thin steel tubing, being stressed only longitudinally and not subjected to bending stresses, gives the car excellent torsional rigidity. Compared with other types of frames, it has the additional advantage of very light weight, which makes itself impressively felt by lightning acceleration and almost breath-taking, high top speed. The very compact streamlined body, which is a light-weight construction, is securely fastened to this frame, and the two form one rigid integral unit.

Light, rigid, and safe

on the New York show stand – as *Road & Track* described it, 'a new car from an old star'.

As a full production car, the new 300SL coupé, not surprisingly, was a sensation. It was recognizably derived from the all-conquering racer of less than two years before, and far from being toned down it now offered even more power and performance, and an even better chassis. The claimed performance figures would make it quite comfortably the fastest true production car in the world.

It kept the same basic engine as derived from the popular 300 saloon, with identical 85.0 × 88.0mm bore and stroke dimensions for the same 2,996cc capacity. The seven-

bearing crank gave the same bottom-end strength and, like the racers, the production car engine had the exotic-for-the-time specification of dry-sump lubrication.

A WORLD FIRST

It also had direct fuel injection which was a world first for a production car, but maybe that should not have come as a total surprise given Daimler-Benz's enthusiastic experimentation with it in the past. That stretched back as far as the early 1930s on aero engines, and Mercedes had even tried injection on cars before the war on the dominant GP racers.

In *Motor Racing* magazine in December 1954, discussing the W196 GP cars, Dr Nallinger and Rudi Uhlenhaut both sang the praises of injection and revealed the depth of experience the company had of its use. Nallinger explained:

It was Daimler-Benz who some time ago introduced petrol injection for aero engines. One may ask why petrol injection should be of advantage as against the use of carburettors, particularly as it is initially more expensive and also, in the case of a four-stroke engine its justification is not as obvious as might appear in the case of a two-stroke engine.

Modern racing engines are invariably high-revving and in the lower speed range are usually what is commonly termed 'hollow'. Their best performance is reached above 50 per cent to 70 per cent of maximum revolutions, thus only giving high performance at a relatively high speed. In consequence of this consideration it was to be expected that the four-stroke engine, with a wide speed range, could be made to maintain a more even range of power if the correct amount of petrol were injected into each cylinder at all speeds. More power at all speeds should be the result.

Furthermore, injection of a measured quantity of petrol into each cylinder ensures the even working of all cylinders, making it possible to obtain from each the maximum load always. From this there would be better power output per cylinder and therefore from the entire engine. By elimination of the usual resistance in the carburettor intake there is full charging of the cylinders, so that maximum performance is really obtained.

Petrol injection also promised more economical consumption figures . . . Moreover, the lower the consumption the less weight has to be carried in fuel . . .

Uhlenhaut went on to point out that:

From extensive use of petrol injection during the war Mercedes found that the system had the effect of upgrading the octane rating of the fuel. With racing fuels it then becomes possible to employ higher compression ratios . . . the reason for the relatively poor performance of the orthodox racing engine, at low revs per minute, was that to get sufficient air into the engine at high speed the choke had to be so large that at low speed there was insufficient air velocity to pick up the fuel from the jets. With injection, the supply of fuel was unaffected by the intake air velocity. In practice, Mercedes racing cars achieved a consumption of 35 litres per 100 kilometres (8.1mpg), the fuel was injected at pressures lower than in diesel engines and the pumps were perfectly reliable. There is a separate lubricating supply to the pump so that no oil need be added to the fuel.

HEAD CHANGES

All the same advantages that Nallinger and Uhlenhaut had quoted for the competition engines (confirmed, of course, by the tests on the late 300SL racers) were equally relevant to the high-performance road car, but the change was not just a case of taking the old carburettors off and bolting the new injection on; some fairly extensive re-engineering was required around the top of the engine.

In fact, the shape of the M186's combustion chambers (with the flat cylinder head surface, and the combustion space formed in the cylinder and defined by the shape of the piston crown) was well suited to adopting injection. The change also gave an opportunity to tackle one of the racer's bad points – the inaccessibility of the spark plugs on the lower side of the steeply canted block. That just would not have been acceptable for a road car with its need for reasonably easy service access. Moving the plugs into a slightly more conventional location alongside the ports in the cylinder head would not only solve the service problem but would also leave a logical place for the injector nozzles in the side of the block.

The jets were aimed into the deepest area of combustion space almost directly below the nose of the plug, and only air, of course, now entered the cylinders via the inlet tracts. The normal manifold was replaced by three pairs of curved ram pipes, joined by a single large plenum chamber with the throttle body at its forward end. Where the stubby inlets necessary to accommodate the old downdraught carbs had given very little ram effect, the long, new air inlet tracts (17in pipes with a minimum internal diameter of 1½in) made a worthwhile contribution – at its best between 5,000 and 6,000rpm. They also helped smooth uneven pulses.

The injection part of the Bosch system was purely mechanical and very similar to a typical diesel layout. The plunger-type pump was mounted on the 'low' side of the engine, and driven at half engine speed by a shaft from the cam-drive end of the engine. A low-pressure electric pump delivered fuel from the tank, through a pre-filter to a mechanical high-pressure pump (and final filter) incorporated in the injector-pump body and driven by the shaft. Internal gears then turned a small camshaft in the pump body whose lobes operated the six plungers, with the correct sequence and timing.

The volume of fuel delivered was controlled at each plunger by an overspill port; the amount of fuel bled away was determined by a slotted sleeve which was controlled by the accelerator linkage and turned as the accelerator was moved. The throttle to admit air to the plenum was also linked directly to the accelerator, so there was always a direct and precise relationship between air and fuel delivery. There was also a thermometer and an altitude compensator system to correct for air temperature and density, but the choke for cold starting was still a manual one. In 1956, the system on the 300SL was further

improved by adopting a vacuum control between the throttle and the fuel governors, which made the delivery more accurate as it now took at least partial note of mass airflow rather than only throttle position. When the car was launched, the injection system was reckoned to add around £60 over the cost of a carburettor engine (equivalent to some £700 in 1992 terms), but Mercedes expected the price to come down quickly enough for injection to be viable on lesser cars in the foreseeable future.

The exhaust headers, which formerly had swept up over the front frame tubes, now curved under the injection trunking, with a big, flat aluminium sheet heat shield sandwiched between the two. The production 300SL engine also had its compression ratio increased to 8.6:1 (although it was still expected to run on 80-octane petrol), and it produced 240bhp at 6,100rpm and 217lb ft of torque at 4,800rpm. It was reportedly quite happy to sustain 6,000rpm, and 6,400rpm was permissible in short bursts. In this form it was known as the M198 engine and the car was officially the W198.

The four-speed gearbox had synchromesh on all the forward gears and originally had the rather long lever as on the racers, but after the first fifty-five cars had been built that was replaced by a shorter, remote change. As in the racers, of course, the engine was steeply canted to the left to maintain the aerodynamics, so few reporters doubted Mercedes' claim that the car would exceed 160mph (257kph) on the longest of the optional final drive ratios. That was 3.25:1 compared to the standard 3.64:1, for which a maximum of around 150mph (241kph) was quoted, and there was an intermediate ratio 3.42:1, supposedly good for 155mph (249kph). At the other end of the scale, injection improved flexibility to the extent that the 300SL would plod along without complaint from no more than 16mph (26kph) in top gear, and doyen of road testers John Bolster discovered that the car on standard gearing would

Bucking the 1950s trend for wire wheels, the 300SL came with steel-centred, alloy-rimmed disc wheels; the knock-off fixing was an option.

Proper bumpers at both the front and rear gave the road car's shell a bit more protection than the vulnerable racer's.

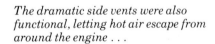

The dramatic side vents were also functional, letting hot air escape from around the engine . . .

. . . and so were the neat 'eyebrows' over the wheelarches – designed to keep the car clean and separate the upper and lower airflows.

The road car's cockpit had not changed a
great deal from the racer's, but it had a
rather more upmarket trim (with leather if
you wanted it), a useful, carpeted luggage
space behind the seats, and even radio
speakers in the pillars.

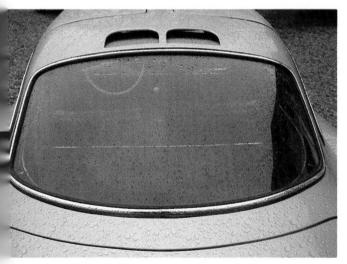

Keeping the driver and passenger cool and
supplied with fresh air was a major concern,
tackled with air intakes ahead of the
windscreen and vents on the trailing edge of
the roof.

An SL body being married to its completed chassis on the Sindelfingen line. Mercedes preferred finned drum brakes to as yet unproven discs.

go from there to 100mph (161kph) in top in 35.2 seconds!

The chassis was directly derived from the racer – an almost identical full spaceframe of small diameter tubes with wishbone front suspension and swing-axle rear suspension. The former still had the secondary vertical mounting pillar for a little more bump compliance and the latter was still the original high-pivot type, without even the lower trailing arms such as had been tried on the racer and which were already in production on the unit-construction 180 saloon. It was one of the few areas where the 300SL would come in for general criticism.

DRUMS, NOT DISCS

With hindsight, one other point of criticism was the brakes, which were the familiar, huge Al-fin units, as used on the racing cars and mounted outboard all round. Disc brakes were definitely the coming thing by the time the 300SL was launched as a production car, and by late 1954 Mercedes had already tested a German-supplied Chrysler disc. Uhlenhaut had also been impressed by Dunlop's hardware when he was planning for the next generation of racing cars, but it would still be some time before Mercedes broke faith with old-fashioned drums – even if they had to supplement them with air brakes for racing.

Most early testers of the 300SL actually raved about how *good* the brakes were, and maybe with their vacuum servo assistance and ample fin-assisted cooling they were by the standards of the day, but the standards were about to change dramatically. Later, having seen just how powerful discs could be, 300SL drivers acknowledged that even the extraordinary lengths that Mercedes went to in design and engineering-for-strength did not quite make up for the basic shortcomings of drums under very heavy use, especially with what had become quite a heavy car.

When disc brakes became available on the Roadster in 1961, some coupé owners converted their cars from drums to discs, but alas only on the front because rear discs were not compatible with the original suspension.

A maximum speed on the far side of 150mph (241kph) also demanded a special tyre choice, because in 1954 the only tyres designed to do that kind of speed were racing ones. Mercedes worked closely with Continental to develop a high-speed road tyre, and one standard option was 6.70 × 15in Continentals on 5½K rims, but racing tyres were often specified too, Dunlop Extra Super Sports being a popular choice.

Like the racers, the 300SL coupé used steel-centred/aluminium-rimmed wheels; a bolt-on type was standard, with a knock-on pattern the optional extra that many SL buyers went for.

PUTTING ON THE STYLE

The essential shape of the 300SL racer had hardly been compromised at all in its metamorphosis into the production 300SL coupé (the wheelbase was the same and the front and rear tracks only marginally changed), but there were enough bits of stylist's whimsy to give it a more finished, more substantial look. Where virtually every panel on the racers had been flat and naked, barely any on the road car were without some sort of subtle adornment. Some of them were practical, some were purely decorative; some were both.

The chrome bumpers were functional of course; even though most of the shell of the standard production car was in steel rather than aluminium, the soft curves of the nose and tail were still vulnerable to clumsy parkers. The doors, boot and bonnet lids were in aluminium, to keep weight down obviously, and that was especially important in the case of the doors as it made them easier to open and close on their assistor struts. The external door pulls were a particularly neat touch; normally the ultra-slim handles lay flush with the bodywork, but when the small raised part at the rear was pushed the full handle pivoted out to unlock the catch and to provide a door-lift.

The huge cooling vents behind the front wheel arches did wonders in visually breaking up the big flat expanse of the racer's sides and they gave a touch of aggression to the styling, but they were functional too. Overheating was frequently a problem on the original SLs, as hot air from under the nose had no easy way to escape once it had passed through the radiator. The big slatted vents solved that problem and with their horizontal chrome strips and forward slant they were a strong styling feature.

In 1953, there had been an interim development car which had had narrower but deeper front vents, set right back near the doors (and with a short exhaust stub emerging from the lower part of the right-hand one), plus small vents just behind the rear arch. The squarer wheelarch openings and a window layout with chrome finisher strips (but no quarter lights and just a small ventilation panel) suggest it was racer-derived. However, the twin bumps had already appeared on the bonnet and so had the neat ventilation intake just ahead of the windscreen, plus

The exceptional aerodynamic cleanness of the 300SL is perhaps clearest of all in the view most people saw.

the outlets on the trailing edge of the roof. The nose and grille were squarer than on any of the racers, with the horizontal chrome bar supporting the three-pointed star, but there was no chrome grille surround and the chrome-rimmed headlights were slightly recessed into the wings and ever so slightly raked back above rectangular turn indicators. The rear lights were on a small flare in the tail, at what later became bumper height, and they looked very vulnerable indeed. The trim strips along the lower sills had appeared, but there were no bumpers yet, no external door handles and no badges. Nor had the 'eyebrows' above the

wheelarches yet appeared, and although the car already looked good, the finalized production version would look even better.

Those distinctive 'eyebrows' which appeared above the wheelarch openings on the final design also mix form and function. They lowered the slab-sided look visually, kept the upper body clean and gave a hint of speed even when the car was stationary. Their aerofoil profile suggests that Mercedes were not being entirely fanciful when they said that the small strakes were really there to separate upper and lower body airflows. The wings were now in steel, so they certainly were not there to add stiffness.

The two small humps in the bonnet were nominally there to clear the top of the cam cover and the offset intake plenum chamber, but in fact only one was really needed for the plenum; the other was added just to balance the appearance. They also happened to relieve the rather austere flatness of the racer's bonnet line – just as the simple chrome outline to the grille and the horizontal bar bearing the big chrome star transformed the nose into something much more stylish and less utilitarian.

There was chrome around the headlights and the indicator lamp bezels, too, in the window finisher strips and even along what on a normal car would have been the sill level.

The 'sill' on the 300SL coupé, of course, was half-way up the side of the car, because the one thing that had not changed in the styling was the famous door layout, and so the 300SL coupé was destined forever to be known and loved as the 'Gullwing'.

TOUCHES OF LUXURY

Like the racing cars, the production model treated driver and passenger to a fair degree of luxury for such an uncompromisingly sporty car – a lot more so, for instance, than most contemporaneous Ferraris, which were still not much more than thinly disguised racers. You still had to climb in over the high sills, but at least the sills were upholstered, and the big steering wheel could be tilted flat (instead of removed altogether as on the racing cars) to make it a bit easier for

The steering wheel was tiltable now rather than being fully removable, and the car was fully trimmed.

Boot space was not a great SL feature.

generously proportioned drivers to ease themselves into the cockpit. Mainly because of the tilt of the engine, left-hand drive only was the order of the day, whatever the market.

The driver's seat was adjustable backwards and forwards but surprisingly the back rake was fixed. Standard seat trim was the distinctive 'tartan' cloth which the racers had used, but leather was an option and was used to finish the dashboard top and other exposed areas, although the dash panel itself was simply painted metal.

The clear instrument layout reflected Mercedes' racing experience; high set and dead ahead of the driver were a large, matching 160mph (257kph) speedometer and 7,000rpm rev-counter; lower down were oil temperature and pressure gauges, water temperature gauge, fuel gauge, and in the middle of the dash, a clock. The switchgear was pretty widely scattered, from the choke and (rarely used) timing adjustment controls on the far left to an additional horn way over to the right in front of the passenger! There was also a switch for an auxiliary electrical fuel pump, which occasionally had to be called on to help with warm starting, which was one of the injection system's weaker points. The handbrake was down

Even as a full production model, the SL was mainly hand-built, with the emphasis on quality control.

Demonstrator par excellence; *Uhlenhaut at the wheel.*

The inevitable development – but not such a simple change as it might have looked at first glance.

between the driver's seat and outer sill, and there were grab handles near the fronts of the doors on both sides – although why the driver needed one was not entirely clear . . .

Obviously remembering the amount of heat the big six-cylinder engine could churn into the cockpit, Mercedes paid particular attention to the ventilation system. There was a double bulkhead between the engine and passenger compartment, and air from a grille just ahead of the windscreen passed through that and out through the side grilles. The main cockpit ventilation consisted of air picked up outboard of the radiator and ducted through a series of vents which were individually controllable by the driver and passenger. Twin extractors were let into the trailing edge of the roof line, and there was a conventional heater system, all of which garnered a lot of praise for being virtually the equal of any prestige saloon system.

The gullwing doors did not allow for winding windows, but the main side panes were removable (and stowable in a bag behind the seats) and there were opening quarter windows. A proper demister system was included too, plus windscreen washers and two-speed wipers.

There was not much by way of luggage space under the normal boot lid, which was where the fuel tank, spare wheel and tools lived (and where you had to go to find the fuel filler), but there was a reasonable amount of space behind the seats, and Mercedes also offered a two-suitcase fitted luggage set and retaining straps. It was not impossible, of course, for the neatly trimmed space behind the rear seats to accommodate one small, hardy, transversely mounted child for very short journeys . . .

WELL RECEIVED

On its launch, *Road & Track* welcomed the car with the comment, 'The production Mercedes-Benz 300SL automobile sets new engineering standards by its unusual combination of ultra-high performance, remarkable roadability, great attention to comfort, extreme flexibility and reasonable price', the last of which they quoted as 'under $7,000'.

In fact, the original list price in the USA (where virtually all the early cars went) was $6,820, and as well as Hoffman's dealership there were three others to cover the country: Inter-Continental Motors, in San Antonio, Texas; Riviera Motors Inc, in San Francisco; and International Motors Inc, on Sunset Boulevard, Hollywood. By normal production car standards, the 300SL, even at what the magazines implied was a surprisingly *low* price, was *very* expensive; yet even at that level, Mercedes were probably making a loss on each car, particularly considering the way the 300SL was manufactured. It was not exactly hand built, but the Sindelfingen production line placed more emphasis on quality than on speed of completion, and there were far more than the usual number of inspection procedures.

Once production was under way, Mercedes would be building some fifty cars a month, but in November 1954 *Motor Sport* reported that the rate had then reached only twenty-five a month, and when *Road & Track* went to Sindelfingen the same November, they photographed 'body number 100' on the line, so the start-up must have been even slower. At that point too, *Motor Sport* reported that Mercedes planned to build 500 cars in all, which would have qualified the car for GT racing, but it was soon clear that they would sell more than that. In fact the official figures record 146 coupés built in 1954, 867 in 1955, 300 in 1956 and 76 in 1957.

Surprisingly perhaps, Mercedes were not quick to let the cars out to the press, but when *Road & Track* got round to testing one (and a privately owned one, at that) a full year after the launch, they were notably enthusiastic:

Few cars have been so long anticipated or so long awaited as the first genuine sports car from Mercedes in over 20 years. Oftentimes a long wait also serves as a cooling off period and the initial trial turns out to be anticlimactic if not completely disillusioning.

In this case, just when we were beginning to suspect that the 300SL coupé would prove to be a mediocre performer, we got one for a full scale road test. The new car turned out to be far beyond our boldest expectations. In fact, we can state unequivocally that in our opinion the 300SL coupé is the ultimate in an all-round sports car. It combines more desirable features in one streamlined package than we ever imagined or hoped would be possible.

Uhlenhaut, naturally enough, had been driving development 300SLs himself since the start of the programme – including another version of the 'interim' car mentioned earlier, this one with wider front vents and the exhaust emerging below the right one in the lower sill. In October 1954, just before the Earls Court Motor Show, he gave the production car its first outing in Britain, demonstrating it to selected members of the press at Silverstone by first taking them out in the passenger seat and then allowing them a few laps of their own. To a man, they were suitably impressed both by Uhlenhaut's legendary skill as a driver and by the 300SL itself – although most implied that its swing-axle handling demanded respect around its limits. Having driven the car from Stuttgart to Silverstone, Uhlenhaut then took it on to Barcelona for the Spanish GP . . .

A TRUE GRAND TOURER

That was the sort of car the 300SL coupé was; not just the fastest production car in the world in its day, but also a perfectly practical, long-distance, high-speed tourer that would take two people and a reasonable amount of luggage all the way across Europe in a day, and still leave them fresh enough to enjoy dinner.

And that was the way it stayed throughout its production life, with very few changes and only minimal options on offer. Of those, the principal ones were the knock-on wheels, a 'competition' camshaft for slightly more power, and an all-aluminium body for slightly less weight. The latter in particular, which saved around 180lb (82kg), was aimed principally at the customers who also raced their 300SLs. In fact very few of the lighter cars were built – only some twenty-nine from a total production of 1,400 coupés between 1954 and 1957. Although the coupé had some impressive competition successes (as described separately) it was a road car first and foremost, and almost before the last one had been built (and the price had climbed from the original $6,820 to $8,905) it was being described as an all-time classic.

ENTER THE ROADSTER

In March 1957, at the Geneva Show, Mercedes took the next logical step and introduced the open-topped Roadster version of the 300SL – an obvious move for the sun-soaked American market, but equally popular even in less clement Europe, and offering a convenient opportunity to put right some of the failings of the original model. That made the Roadster a great deal more than just a coupé with the top chopped off; it was heavily redesigned almost from the ground up, starting with the chassis itself, to maintain stiffness and add convenience.

Two things dictated that change. First, an open-topped car is never as stiff as a closed one, so some additional strengthening around the cockpit opening is always desirable. Second, distinctive though the gullwing door arrangement was, it had always had its critics as well as its admirers – particularly among ladies in skirts. In the pre-equality

The large hole created by chopping off the roof made space for an elegant open-plan office, but meant Mercedes had to add stiffness elsewhere . . .

. . . so the spaceframe chassis was comprehensively revised . .

. . . even allowing for proper doors above much lower but still immensely strong sill structures.

There are disc brakes on all four wheels, tuned to the performance and speed of the 300 SL. A light pressure on the brake pedal – effectively increased by the vacuum booster – will bring the full power of

the brakes into action. The single pivot swing axle, equipped with a compensating spring, ensures optimum road-holding and cornering.

The tubular lattice frame is a characteristic of modern design. The tubes are subjected only to pull or pressure and not to bending forces – the main reason for its stability and absolute torsion resistance. The light-weight bodywork is screwed onto the frame to form an integral unit. This entire power plant as well as the wheel mounting linkage are flexibly mounted. This feature, together with the single point swing axle, accounts for the perfect coordination of the chassis units. The Mercedes-Benz recirculating ball-type steering is extremely responsive and easy to handle.

The 'single-pivot' rear suspension (above which can be seen the compensating spring) improved handling dramatically, and Mercedes finally offered disc brakes.

Engine architecture remained essentially unchanged, but a sportier cam, higher compression and more power compensated for the Roadster's additional weight.

Here you can clearly see the oblique angle of the engine. The flat head was dependent upon this unusual arrangement, also beneficial for vision directly in front of the car.

A fully wrap-around windscreen was one of the major styling changes on the Roadster . . .

. . . the side vents gained some dramatic chrome 'speed-stripes' . . .

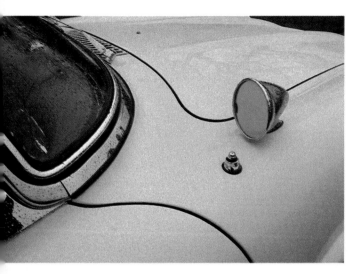

. . . and the separate round headlight and sidelight layout was replaced by these huge vertical units.

The wheelarch 'eyebrows' remained, and it was normal to have neat hubcaps finished in body colour.

mid-1950s it was remarkable how many of the male testers of the SL coupé made jolly little asides about the stirring sight of a young lady making her entrance or exit over the high, wide sill; always into the passenger seat, of course, as the 'lucky guest' of the owner, who it was taken for granted would be a red-blooded male . . .

Accordingly, the Roadster chassis, while essentially similar to that of the coupé, had additional bracing in the centre section above the transmission tunnel but much lower side members, which allowed for conventional, front-hinging doors above normal height sills. Even more importantly, although it retained the usual double wishbone front suspension, it had a heavily reworked rear suspension, as already introduced with great success on Mercedes' latest generation of unit-construction saloon cars, and even on the supposedly less exotic 190SL. The aim of the new suspension, of course, was to rid the Roadster of some of the twitchier rear-end handling characteristics of the coupé.

TAMING THE OVERSTEER

It was still a swing-axle system, but now it was a 'low-pivot' type rather than the old 'high pivot'. It went one step beyond the high-pivot axle with lower trailing arms as used on the 180 saloon and tried on the late 300SL racers.

The main feature of the new design was that it simultaneously lowered the pivot point and increased the length of the swinging arms by introducing a single articulation point below the final drive unit, and virtually at the centre of the track. Typically, Mercedes tried it first on a racing car, back-to-back with various other possibilities, including double-articulated types and other double-low-pivot designs. The single-low-pivot layout proved best for both roadholding and ride comfort, and was adopted for the 220 series production

cars, the W196 GP car and the closely related 300SLR racers, plus the 190SL, even before it went on to the new Roadster.

For the production cars, the suspension had three mounting points. The final drive unit mounted at a single, central point (via a substantial rubber block) to the chassis; inside the differential housing, there was a universal joint to the right of the differential itself, allowing the two half-axles to move independently, and there was a sliding joint within one shaft to accommodate the small changes in length as the shafts moved through their arcs.

Where the two half-axles previously pivoted at a point in line with their long axis, the new system extended the outer casings of the half-axles downwards and pivoted them together at a single point approximately below the crownwheel and pinion, so both axles would now swing from that much lower and further inboard. The other two mountings were the outboard coil spring and telescopic damper units. One later refinement was added when a third 'compensating' spring was mounted transversely between the axles across the pivot, to give better control of body roll in hard cornering but without affecting normal spring rate.

In practical terms, the low-pivot axle transformed the handling of the car quite dramatically, making it much more user-friendly around its limits. It also usefully reduced its tendency to snap into terminal oversteer as roll increased the rear camber angles, or especially if the driver lifted off the power too suddenly in mid-corner. With the low-pivot axle, the basic geometrical effect was still there (Mercedes still believed in a slight degree of oversteer as the most desirable balance), but to a much more acceptable degree.

Another significant improvement on the Roadster over the coupé was in the steering, which had its ratio reduced from only around two turns lock-to-lock to around three; that both made the steering a bit lighter at low speeds and took away some of the over-sensitivity that could frighten the lesser driver. Michelin X radial tyres were now standard fitting too, and they improved the road feel and the ride comfort, although they did have a reputation for being rather 'sudden' when they finally did break away – this was a real problem with early radials and one which Mercedes had the tyre manufacturers confront in planning for the next generation of SLs.

MORE POWER, MORE WEIGHT, MORE MONEY

All the 300SL Roadsters used what had been known as the 'competition' camshaft option on the coupé, and had a higher compression ratio (at 9.5:1 rather than 8.6:1) which took the quoted power output to 250bhp at 6,200rpm and peak torque to 228lb ft at 5,000rpm. That was not quite enough to offset the higher weight (by a couple of hundred pounds) of the Roadster though, and even with a revised standard axle ratio (of 3.89:1 rather than 3.64:1) the open car was never quite as accelerative as the coupé. Naturally, too, with its inferior aerodynamics it was markedly slower in top speed; about 125–130mph (201–209kph) was typically quoted.

Ultimate performance was no longer the real point of the 300SL by the time it had reached the Roadster stage. As *Road & Track* said in 1961, testing one of the later cars:

The interior appointments of the 300SL are in keeping with the five-figure price tag and have successfully separated this car from the category of stark functionalism fitting the die-hard sports car enthusiast's ideas of what a sports car should be. Due to the car's de luxe interior, and the relatively heavy weight (which is rather far afield from the company's designation of SL, meaning

Super Light) we would actually classify the 300 as a Grand Touring car, rather than a sports car. And what grand touring it is!

That was true enough. The cockpit was obviously different from that of the coupé in that it had much lower sills and so felt a bit more roomy, the dashboard had changed in detail layout (with the minor instruments between the speedo and rev-counter and with more modern switches) and the preferred seat trim was now leather. It even had wind-up windows, which in American terminology made it a convertible rather than a roadster – this implied something a bit more spartan, with only side curtains and no hood.

The soft-top, in typical Mercedes fashion, was a superb fit, beautifully trimmed inside with a full lining, and extremely easy to raise and lower. It stowed neatly when down, under a hinged metal panel behind the seats where the coupé's luggage used to go. Fortunately, by reshaping the fuel tank and moving the spare wheel under the boot floor, Mercedes had created some worthwhile space in the tail where the coupé had none.

There were a few styling changes on the Roadster too, notably a more curved windscreen, extended chrome 'speed-lines' through the side vents and along the doors, and deep, new one-piece front light units, which incorporated the headlights, foglights and turn indicators. Mercedes called them *Lichteinheit*, or unity lights. They gave the Roadster a slightly less aggressive look than the coupé, but it was still a delightful design.

The 'five-figure price tag' that *Road & Track* referred to later was five figures right from the start, and their first encounter in January 1958 listed it at $10,970.

That did not stop it outselling the coupé in a production life that lasted into 1963. In successive years from its 1957 launch until then, it sold 554, 324, 211, 249, 250, 244 and 26 copies respectively, for an overall total of

The Roadster was an exceptionally handsome car, and it looked every bit as good with the soft-top raised . . .

. . . or when wearing the optional hard-top.

1,858 cars. To put that into perspective though, while Mercedes made a total of 3,264 SLs between 1952 and 1963, including the original racers, they made some 455,000 cars in the 220 series between 1951 and 1965, at a rate of up to 65,000 a year in a good year . . .

Yet the SLs were always the glamour cars. In 1958 the Roadster offered the desirable option of a lift-off hard-top (which could all

As before, the badges said it all, and there were no additional letters for the Roadster.

but turn it into a coupé for winter use but at the expense of even more weight) and in March 1961 it finally gained disc brakes all round – Dunlop units, all mounted outboard.

By now, though, the 300SL was nearing the end of its usefulness to Mercedes, who had gained plenty of prestige from the model over the years but very little profit. They had also pulled out of racing completely after the 1955 Le Mans tragedy when Levegh's 300SLR crashed into the crowd, and their sporting image was giving way to one more strongly emphasizing quality. There was still room in the range for a sporty car, but less overtly so, and when the next family of SLs was launched in 1963 it was based on a saloon car floorpan, and sacrificed ultimate performance for even more luxury and the chance of making a decent profit at last . . .

The racing SLRs

It may be stretching things a little to include the 300SLR in the SL story, but the badge alone gives it a place, even though in reality it was related to no other car in the series and was in effect not much more than a sports-bodied GP car.

It was first cousin to the W196 single-seater, as campaigned on the GP trail in 1954 and 1955. During those two years, the W196 won both world championships. The 300SLR racing sports car was raced for just one year – 1955 – during which it comprehensively beat all-comers to the World Championship for Sports Cars, and in which the only time it failed to win was when it was withdrawn from Le Mans under the most tragic of circumstances.

Where the GP car was limited by the regulations to 2½ litres, the 300SLR was a full 3 litres, and where the W196 was a single-seater (even when run with the sports-car-like all-enveloping streamliner body), the SLR was nominally always a two-seater – and sometimes genuinely a two-seater. Those basic differences apart, the two cars were clearly two variations on the same state-of-the-art theme.

Like the racing and production 300SLs, the 300SLR had a complex but light and immensely stiff spaceframe chassis, although it was an open car with no call to meet rules on doors – it did not need any gullwing-type trickery. The frame was even lighter than the production SL's at just 132lb (60kg), and the entire car was reckoned to weigh considerably less than 2,000lb (907kg) without fuel or driver.

Front suspension was by wishbones; rear suspension introduced the low-pivot swing-axle layout, with a Watts linkage for additional location. The springing medium at both ends was torsion bars, and at the rear they were linked to the swinging axles by short lever arms.

To give the best possible weight distribution within the stubby wheelbase, the weight of the long engine at the front was balanced by putting the combined five-speed transmission and final-drive at the back, below a massive fuel tank sculpted to fill every available bit of space.

The brakes were still drums, massive Al-fin units and mounted inboard at the front and rear to minimize unsprung weight, while using the turbine-like alloy fins and clever shrouding to give excellent cooling. Four mysterious knobs below the dash could each squirt a fine film of oil into a chosen brake drum to prevent sticking after repeated hard applications.

For the fastest circuits, Mercedes revived the air-brake theme first tried at Le Mans in practice in 1952 on the 300SLs, but this time they made it work supremely well. The movable flap was in the rear body deck behind the driver, complete with head fairing. It was controlled by a simple lever in the cockpit and was operated hydraulically from a pump-driven high-pressure circuit. Most of the drivers simply used the huge flap to complement the drum brakes at very high speeds (which it did brilliantly), but Moss, as Uhlenhaut was most impressed to note, used it additionally to trim the car's handling balance in very fast corners.

For all the brilliant chassis engineering, the most impressive part of the whole car was probably

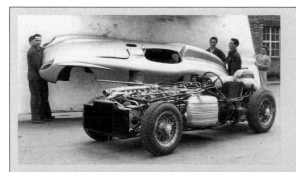

A super-sophisticated chassis and engine, and ultra-light, ultra-slippery bodyshell were the keys to dominance.

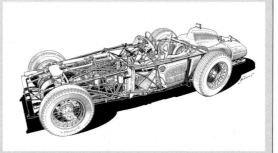

The single-seater W196 GP car was the starting point for the 300SLR sports racers.

State of the art and Mercedes-style in 1955 — including fuel-injected, desmo-valved engine, inboard front brakes and wishbone-plus-torsion-bar suspension.

Although they did not yet use discs (or perhaps because they did not) Mercedes did persist with air brakes.

(Right) Not much more than a two-seater GP car. Lightness was everything.

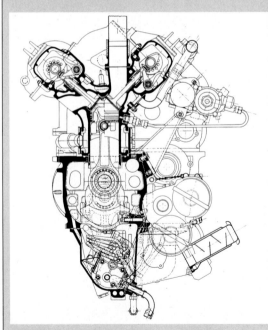

One of the all-time-great racing engines, derived from the W196 for the 300SLR, and capable of producing some 100bhp/litre.

Fangio with the air brake in action at Le Mans 1955, but Moss was reckoned to be the true master of its subtleties.

Battered but still beautiful; a works 300SLR driven by Peter Collins in the 1955 Targa Florio. He shared with Stirling Moss, and they won of course.

the GP-derived straight-eight, twin-cam engine. It shocked some people when it appeared, in so far as a straight-eight seemingly threatens more disadvantages than advantages – bulk, complexity, awkward vibrational problems and more – but Mercedes once again conquered theory with pure engineering excellence.

In effect, rather than a true straight-eight, it was a pair of fours running end-to-end, with power taken off from the centre of the common crankshaft. Where the GP engine had fabricated barrels welded up into the four-cylinder blocks, the SLR engine had cast aluminium blocks. Like the GP car, however, the heads were integral with the blocks and the whole assembly was spigotted into the lower crankcase.

The valves were at the widest possible angle – over 90 degrees – set symmetrically about the centre-line of the bores, above very high-domed pistons. The desmodromic system meant that cams both opened and closed the valves without springs – to allow maximum revs in conjunction with the roller-bearing crankshaft and rods.

For the sports car it had grown from the short-stroke 76.0 × 68.8mm of the 2½-litre GP car to an exactly square 78.0 × 78.0mm and 2,982cc. It retained the well-proven Bosch direct injection and a dry-sump system, with a massive tank at the front left of the chassis. The engine was tilted at some 35 degrees for the usual aerodynamic and centre of gravity advantages. Even for endurance racing, in a conservative state of tune it produced at least 276bhp at 7,000rpm; more normally it gave as much as 300bhp at some 7,400rpm, and some 220lb ft of torque at 6,000rpm which meant the five-speed gearbox needed to be worked quite hard.

As in the GP car, the 300SLR driver sits astride the propellor shaft, but that aside, every aspect of the cockpit layout was designed to cater for driver comfort. The seat was made to measure and trimmed for long-distance coolness, the steering wheel was removable at the push of a button for easier entry and exit at rapid pit-stops, and even the steering ratio could be varied to suit driver preference.

In action, the 300SLR simply steamrollered the opposition throughout the 1955 racing season.

The most famous victory, perhaps, was in the Mille Miglia, where Stirling Moss won with motoring journalist Denis Jenkinson in the passenger seat. The bearded, bespectacled Jenkinson, as well as being one of the world's most respected motor sports writers, was far more than regulatory ballast in the SLR. He devised a system of pace notes, written on to a 17ft (5m) long strip of paper and describing every salient feature of the course, noted and refined over long days of flat-out reconnaissance.

During the race he ran the paper roll between two rollers in a small metal box, past a slot through which he could read the notes. He then passed the information on to Moss by a series of hand signals, and on the strength of the 'pace notes' Moss was able to maintain maximum speed even when the road was effectively blind.

Moss won the race by more than half an hour from Fangio in a second 300SLR. Three 300SLs, led home by John Fitch, gave Mercedes a 1-2-3 finish in the hugely competitive GT class, and five cars in the top ten. Moss's winning average was almost 10mph (16kph) faster than the previous record, and was never beaten in the remaining couple of years before the race was outlawed as being too dangerous.

As for the rest of the year, Fangio and Moss finished first and second in the Swedish sports car round; Moss/Fitch, Fangio/Kling and von Trips/Simon/Kling took first, second and third in the Ulster TT; and Moss with Peter Collins won the Targa Florio, from Fangio and Kling.

The only desperate damper on an outstanding year was at Le Mans. Three cars were entered and by around 6.30 a.m. on Sunday morning Fangio's car was disputing the lead with Mike Hawthorn's D-Type Jaguar, with the Ferrari challenge fading. Then Pierre Levegh, hero of the 1952 race and guest driving one of the 300SLRs, collided with Lance Macklin's Austin Healey as Macklin moved over to avoid Hawthorn who was headed into the pits. Levegh's SLR was launched off the sloping tail of the Healey, over the low barriers and into the crowd in the main stands opposite the pits and start line. The Mercedes exploded in flames, sending wreckage scything through the crowd. Levegh and over eighty spectators were killed in the worst racing accident in history. Some hours later, when Fangio and Moss were leading by two laps and clearly set for victory, Neubauer withdrew his two remaining cars as a mark of respect.

At the end of the year, Mercedes withdrew from racing completely. But for the Le Mans accident they might have continued with the sports car for a while longer, but as before, they had proved just about all there was to prove, so it was by no means a certainty.

The SLRs were retired. None had been built for a private owner and none was sold subsequently. Two had been built as very 300SL-like coupés, but distinguished by stub exhausts from the mighty straight-eight exiting from the vents in the body side. Uhlenhaut used one as his personal transport for some time, and late in 1956 Gordon Wilkins drove the car for *Motor Racing* magazine and recorded the highest speed ever in a magazine road test up to that time, with a best run at exactly 180mph (290kph). Sadly, he also recorded that this ultimate SL was not for sale and never would be.

5 An Affordable Alternative: The 190SL

Basking in the reflected glory of the 300SL Gullwing coupé at its launch in New York in January 1954 was another Mercedes sports car. It had something of the look of the 300 around its nose, it sat on the same wheelbase and it seemed almost as big all round, but under the skin this neat little two-seater convertible was really baby brother.

It was an important baby brother though. Where the 300SL had started life as Uhlenhaut's project for bringing Mercedes back into motor sport, and as such had been less concerned with commercial considerations than with winning races and building an image, this other car was Nallinger's baby, and its sole purpose was to sell well and make money.

It was called the 190SL, and in spite of its obviously more modest specification, it was clearly intended to capitalize on the bigger *Sport Licht*'s already well-established reputation and open it up to a different and more numerous customer level.

It was a clever piece of aspirational marketing and a clever piece of engineering too. Under the racy skin, the 190SL was a far simpler car than the spaceframed, fuel-injected, gullwinged 300, and it used even more production-based components. Once on line, it would be relatively easy and economical to build in respectable volumes — which to a manufacturer means respectable profits. And although it still would not exactly be cheap by other people's standards, it would certainly look like an attractive proposition

for anyone wanting to buy on to the first rung of the Mercedes sporting ladder. As it stood in the New York exhibition hall, Mercedes were quoting the tantalizingly close-to-reachable price of 'less than $4,000' – compared to almost $7,000 for the 300 coupé. In its way it was almost as interesting as big brother . . .

Yet the strange thing was, it seems to have taken everybody by surprise. The press and even the public had long been expecting the 300SL to make the transition from racer to road car, and the package was similar enough to the famous racers so that it felt almost familiar by the time it was unveiled. However, the 190 was a different proposition – nobody had had any inkling that it was coming.

PRODUCTION BASE

Its all-steel roadster body clothed a mixture of existing and new components brilliantly used. The biggest difference from the 300SL in terms of making the 190SL mass-producable was in the chassis. Where the coupé had the complex, frighteningly expensive and inevitably largely hand-built spaceframe, the 190SL (which appeared first as a simple convertible but was eventually to be offered as an open car with the choice of a soft-top, a hard-top or both) took Mercedes further down the modern road of unitary constuction, in which the body and floorpan in

Für sportliches Fahren
auf Sonderwunsch mit Sporttüren aus Leichtmetall
und Sportscheibe

Zur weiteren Gewichtsverminderung
können die Stoßstangen und auch das
Verdeck abgeschraubt werden

*'For sporting drivers'; even if the 190SL was only a baby brother of the mighty
300s, Mercedes intended to emphasize that it was a sports car – even occasionally
usable as a weekend racer.*

effect *were* the chassis. It was only Mercedes'
second model to use this form of construction
and it was closely based on the first.

That was the 180 saloon (type W120 in
Mercedes-speak), as launched in 1953. The
180 was the most compact and cheapest of
the Mercedes saloons, and a modern technology replacement for the 170 – the car which
had helped Mercedes back into production in
the late 1940s but which had actually been
no more than a revamped pre-war model.

The 180 started life with the 170's venerable 1.8-litre, four-cylinder, side-valve
engine, but otherwise it was all new. It
had been two years in the making and it
was thoroughly up to date, not only in its
new engineering, but also in its styling and
packaging. That took advantage of the new
unitary construction method to provide substantially more passenger and luggage
space for less weight and no more external
size.

The floorpan was welded up from sheet
steel pressings, and based its strength on a
substantial centre tunnel and two totally
enclosed, box-type side members. The central structure split into two forks at its front
end, and the ends of the 'Y' were joined
ahead of the engine space by a large, tubular
cross member. The side members curved in
to meet the sides of the fork just aft of the
front suspension, and they were also joined
across the width of the car by four main box-
section cross members, all welded on to the
main floorpan pressings to form a single
structure.

Just behind the passenger area the chassis
narrowed to accommodate the rear suspension and wheels, and the centre tunnel forked
again and swept up to house the final drive
unit. The two parallel box-section outer
members were similarly joined by cross
beams and the sheet metal pan which was
dished at either side of the boot floor to take
two spare wheels if the customer chose.

It was easier to make than the old-style

Smaller it may have been, but the 190 had a lot of the same philosophy of the bigger car, especially in its smooth aerodynamics.

Once into production, the nose shape clearly evoked the 300SL coupé, but just one bonnet bulge showed that something below was not quite the same.

190SL, 1955–63

Body type	:	two-door, two-seater sports roadster with folding soft-top and/or detachable hard-top
Chassis	:	platform with unitary body
Engine type	:	in-line four-cylinder
Capacity	:	1,897cc
Bore	:	85.0mm
Stroke	:	83.6mm
Compression ratio	:	8.5:1
Cylinders	:	cast-iron block, three main bearings
Cylinder head	:	alloy, with two valves per cylinder operated by single, chain-driven, overhead camshaft
Fuel system	:	two twin-choke sidedraught Solex carburettors
Maximum power	:	120bhp at 5,700rpm
Maximum torque	:	107lb ft at 2,800rpm
Bhp per litre	:	63.3
Gearbox type	:	four-speed manual
Gear ratios	:	Fourth: 1.00 Second: 2.32
		Third: 1.52 First: 3.52
		Reverse: 3.52
Final drive ratio	:	3.89:1
Clutch	:	single dry-plate
Front suspension	:	unequal-length double wishbones, coil springs, telescopic dampers, anti-roll bar
Rear suspension	:	low-pivot swing axle, longitudinal arms, coil springs, telescopic dampers
Brakes	:	Al-fin drums all round; with vacuum assistance
Steering	:	recirculating ball
Wheels and tyres	:	steel; 6.40 × 13in cross-ply tyres
Overall length	:	166.1in (421.9cm)
Overall width	:	68.5in (174.0cm)
Overall height	:	52in (132.1cm)
Wheelbase	:	94.5in (240.0cm)
Track	:	56.2in (142.7cm) front; 57.9in (147.1cm) rear
Ground clearance	:	6.1in (15.5cm)
Fuel tank capacity	:	14.3gal (64.9 litres)
Unladen weight	:	2,388lb (1,083kg)
Power to weight ratio	:	112.6bhp/ton

PERFORMANCE

Maximum speed	:	107mph (172kph)
0–60mph (0–97kph)	:	13.3sec
0–100mph (0–161kph)	:	n/a
Standing ¼ mile (0.4km)	:	17.8sec
Fuel consumption	:	approx 22mpg (7.8km per litre)

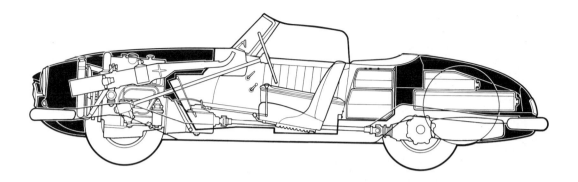

Size was not the only key to selling a 'bargain priced' SL; simplicity was equally important, as the expensive spaceframe gave way to a mass-production platform.

cruciform frames, and was stiffer, lighter and cheaper. With the upper body shell welded on, it became an immensely strong box structure; with it left off it became an ideal starting point for Dr Nallinger's new sports car.

SALOON TO SPORTS CAR

With only two seats to worry about, the 190SL could afford to be even more compact than the five-seater 180. The first move for the engineers was to take the saloon's pressed steel floorpan and lose just over 10in (25cm) out of the wheelbase, to bring that down to the same 94.5in (240cm) as the 300SL coupé. It was then necessary to stiffen what was left to satisfy the notoriously flexible superstructure of an open-topped car. The 180 suspension was grafted on virtually unchanged – which was no great compromise

The donor model for the 190SL was the new 180 saloon – Mercedes' first unit construction car and the start of a whole modern family.

*Mercedes were clever enough to give much of
the interior feel of the 300s to the 190, and
the sporting feel was real.*

*Just like the 180 saloon, the 190SL kept
life simple and economical by combining
engine, transmission and suspension
package on a compact and complete front
subframe.*

Everyone today who frequently travels by car knows from experience that a modern
automobile is only as good as it is safe. Only when the safety can be taken as a matter
of course, as with the 190 SL, can the other advantages be given their true value.

*Smaller wheels were a new trend inherited
from the 180, using new tyre technology and
benefiting handling with a lower centre of
gravity.*

*It could only be a Mercedes; the 190's
typically idiosyncratic dash and control
layout included the familiar steering-wheel-
mounted indicator ring.*

*First appearance for a new engine – the 190's single-overhead-camshaft four-
cylinder engine with 'square' cylinder-head joint and carburettors. (The gearbox
is behind.)*

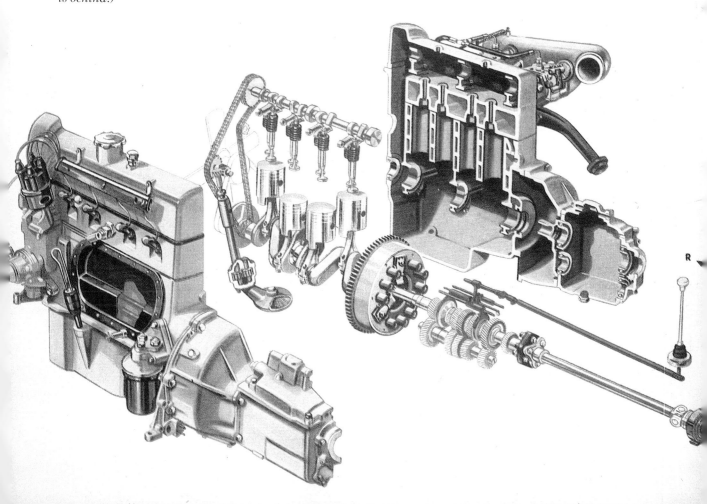

because it was newly designed for the 180 and a big improvement on earlier systems. In fact, at the back in particular, the suspension on the 190SL was clearly superior to that on the original 300SL.

At the front there were the familiar double, unequal-length wishbones with coil springs and telescopic dampers, plus an anti-roll bar. In this case, though, rather than having the intermediate vertical pillars to isolate the body from road shocks, the suspension was mounted on a separate, wishbone-shaped subframe, fabricated from two steel pressings and just the same as on the 180.

The subframe also carried the steering gear and the engine/gearbox assembly, and it was attached to the front chassis forks and forward cross member at three points, all insulated from road shocks by rubber mountings. Mercedes called the subframe the *Fahrschemel,* or front suspension support. As well as its compactness and excellent road insulation, it had the massive advantage of being designed for separate assembly and quick and easy attachment to the completed shell, making the whole production process simpler and cheaper.

At the rear, the 190SL as unveiled at the New York show had the 180's new swing-axle, with rubber-bushed lower trailing arms taking the driving and braking torques forward to the chassis, carrying the coil-spring/damper units so that the final drive housing only needed a single-point mounting instead of the previous four points. It was the system that had been tried at a late stage on the 300SL racers but not adopted for the production 300SL coupé. Although, for the time being at least, it still had the 'high-pivot' swing axles, it was nonetheless a definite improvement over the basic system in that the half-axles were lighter and so the unsprung weight was reduced.

Another bonus came from the fact that, in the modern idiom, the 180 had adopted much smaller diameter wheels than the 170 (13in rather than 16in, and smaller, too,

than the 300SL's 15in type), which reduced unsprung weight even further. The 190SL was able to use the 180's smaller wheels too (still in bolt-on form), and as well as the weight benefits, that also effectively reduced both the centre of gravity and the troublesome roll-height of the original suspension.

In using the same wheels, the 190 also used the 180's tyre size of 6.40 × 13in, these cross-ply tyres having been specially developed for the saloon to give at least comparable wear to the larger diameter ones.

The 190SL also kept the 180's four-speed, all-synchromesh manual gearbox (and even used the column change on the original prototypes). It had outboard drum brakes with twin leading shoe operation (of the same diameter as the 180's because of the small wheels, though a good deal wider than those on the saloon and with added fins for cooling), and it used the recirculating-ball steering with hydraulic damper. It even had a 180-type steering wheel with the classic Mercedes horn ring that also worked the turn indicators and, very un-sports-car-like, it had an umbrella type handbrake lever under the dashboard.

A NEW ENGINE

Even in the 180 saloon, the 170-derived side-valve engine was considered to be long in the tooth and maybe rather out of character with the rest of the new thinking. What is more, it only produced 52bhp at a very unexciting 4,000rpm, which obviously would not be much use for even a smaller and much lighter sports car. So to power the 190SL, Mercedes introduced a new overhead-valve engine – the type M121.

To all intents and purposes it was a four-cylinder version of the single-overhead-camshaft, six-cylinder 300 engine in its original, carburettor guise. The bore was exactly the same, at 85.0mm, but the stroke was reduced very slightly to 83.6mm, which

This time the engine was mounted vertically.

with four cylinders gave a capacity of 1,897cc and made the engine just fractionally over-square. Like the 300s, it had the combustion space in the top of the iron block, chain drive to the camshaft and the two big, offset valves for each cylinder were operated by unequal-length finger rockers in an alloy head. It used a wet sump and a heat exchanger arrange-ment between oil and water in the water jackets to help control oil temperature.

With a compression ratio of 8.5:1 and two sidedraught, twin-choke Solex carburettors, it was impressively powerful and free-revving for its capacity and its day. It was reckoned to be safe to 6,000rpm even though it only had three main bearings. Mercedes initially claimed 125bhp at 5,500rpm (in

SAE terms at least – the European quote with ancillaries in position was 110bhp) and a torque peak of 114lb ft, but those figures varied slightly once the car was launched, the most commonly quoted peak power being 120bhp at 5,700rpm. Carburation modifications once the car was into produc-tion also changed the torque peak to 101lb ft at 3,800rpm and later, with improved flexi-bility, to 105lb ft at 3,200.

Unlike the 300SL's unit, the 190's engine was mounted vertically in the chassis (the car itself was more than 2in (5cm) taller than the coupé), and without the complexities of the injection and the exhaust plumbing or the two extra cylinders it looked a bit less intimidating under the bonnet.

The 190SL was strictly a two-seater, but there was room behind the seats for some luggage, or one tolerant child.

Wind-up door windows were one thing there had never been room for in the 300SL coupé.

The 190SL was well protected front and rear for ordinary use, but the bumpers were supposedly easily removable for weekend racers.

This time, incidentally, the sports car got the engine first and the saloon car inherited it later. The saloon in this case was the 190 which was introduced in 1956 with a single-carburettor version of the engine, giving 84bhp.

With some 40bhp more than that in the 190SL, it still had a fair amount of work to do because the steel-bodied roadster, with all the chassis stiffening implied by the open-top layout, and with generous trim including wind-up windows and a proper heating and ventilating system with individual controls for driver and passenger, was never going to be any lightweight. Even as announced, the standard version was quoted as weighing 2,320lb (1,052kg) with fuel, and by the time the car was actually launched into production, that had gone up even further.

There was a small list of options for those who wanted to go racing at a modest level with their 190s (which would be eligible for the 2-litre Class E sports car category in the USA); they mainly comprised a choice between bench or bucket seats, a plexiglass aero screen to replace the full-width curved windscreen (to cut drag), simplified equipment levels, and lighter doors with a fashionable 'cut-down' shape under the elbows. The top and the bumpers were also easily removable, all of which was said to save 300lb (136kg) or more. Even that was not going to be enough to turn the 190SL into any great roadburner, so its competition career was strictly limited to the weekend hobby fraternity.

It was mainly accepted for what it was: a comfortable, well-trimmed and well-made car with soft-top versatility, adequate straight-line performance and far better than average roadholding, plus, of course, that prestigious three-pointed star on the nose, and the SL connection.

Reporting its début in 1954, *Speed Age* magazine was particularly enthusiastic, declaring, 'The Mercedez-Benz 190SL is a car suited for all purposes, the perfect synthesis of touring and sporting characteristics . . .'

A LONG BUT WORTHWHILE WAIT

Enthusiasm notwithstanding, between the car being announced at the New York show and it actually going into production there was to be a long delay. While the customers waited, that nose changed somewhat, and so did several other details as the car was developed between the factory at Unterturkheim and the circuit at Nurburgring.

Progress was somewhat slowed by the need to develop the W196 GP car and the closely related 300SLR at the same time, but it went ahead gradually. In November 1954, the 190SL was reported as undergoing minor aerodynamic improvements with production expected to start in December, and in fact it did stumble into production in small numbers by January 1955, although supplies were pretty slow until much later in the year. It was first shown off in Europe at the Geneva Motor Show in March 1955, by which time it was more or less into production proper.

In the interim, the 190SL had come to look even more like the 300SL when viewed from head on and it had put on a bit more weight. On the positive side, however, by the time it went into production it had the much improved low-pivot swing axle with single central pivot, which was introduced at more or less the same time on the new 220 saloon series. Look in the boot of a 190SL and you can see the top mounting point for the differential in the middle, up against the rear bulkhead. On the 190, the centre pillar was also given an additional locating strut, running sideways to the chassis to take some of the lateral loads.

Visually, the early version of the car had had a scoop on the bonnet, which was open at the front and used as an air intake; the final design had a neat, rounded bulge which looked a lot nicer. The bonnet itself no longer opened all the way to the grille, and the nose aperture had become a bit more rounded and a lot more attractive. Where the first car had only had the 300SL-type side strakes over the front wheelarches, the production version had them over both front and rear, which made the rear wings appear more smoothly blended into the flanks to give a more modern look. The bumpers had been fitted with overriders.

Inside, the gear-lever had moved from the steering column to where it more properly belonged on a sporting car, on the floor in the centre, which meant that the front bench seat was no longer a feasible option. There was real luggage space in the boot where the 300SL only offered the huge spare wheel, and there was more space behind the seats – enough, in fact, to accommodate an optional occasional (*very* occasional) seat which fitted in across the width of the car. Mercedes offered a set of three fitted cases for the boot and two for behind the front seats which made the car very good on luggage capacity.

The weight had gone up to about 2,500lb and the asking price had gone up slightly too, but it was still under $4,000 basic in the USA – if only just at $3,998. In Britain it cost just over £2,776 (including purchase tax) when John Bolster tested one for *Autosport* in November 1955 and remarked on the desirable 300SL association:

The appearance is very effective, and the lines cannot be faulted. 'My' car was red, with cream upholstery, and it created something of a furore when I drove it in Paris. Naturally I went to visit mine host, Harry Schell, at *L'Action Automobile* . . . and almost succeeded in emptying his bar, so great was the interest in the latest 'Merc'. The marked resemblance of the 190SL to its bigger brother is a great attraction, and the makers have been wise to cash in on the glamour that surrounds the 300SL . . .

COMMERCIAL SUCCESS

Cash in they did, and very usefully too. Not surprisingly, the 190 sold a great deal quicker than the 300SLs, and between 1955 and 1963 when both it and the 300SL Roadster were replaced by a new generation of SL, almost 26,000 190SLs were built – representing a profitable average level of better than 3,000 cars a year.

In all that time there were very few changes, and what few there were were minor. Early on, as already mentioned, the two-stage carburation was slightly modified to improve low speed torque, and as early as 1955 the tall third gear ratio was changed to make better use of it in traffic. The compression ratio was raised to 8.5:1 early on, and again to 8.8:1 around 1960 as better petrol became more common. The rear window in the hard-top versions was made a bit bigger for the 1960 model, to look more like the 300SL Roadster, and that (apart from an ever-increasing price, which had reached over $5,800 by the beginning of 1962) was about all that changed throughout the model's run.

It also stayed very popular with the testers, who occasionally bemoaned the fact that it did not have enough power while simultaneously admitting that they knew that was not the point. They *did* almost universally like the handling, the steering, the brakes and the levels of equipment, although there was also the odd moan about the seats being too firm, not grippy enough and with fiddly adjustment for the back rake. *Sports Car Illustrated*'s comments in late 1958, though, were fairly typical of how well the car was liked:

Daimler-Benz products have a worldwide reputation for absolute reliability and the reputation is deserved if the 190SL which we were privileged to treat as our own for a full month was any criterion.

Everything about the 190SL is designed

In the best Mercedes traditions, the 190SL's styling has stood the test of time well mainly because it was kept simple.

Something to be proud of.

to coddle its possessor. From a top that can be raised or lowered with one hand while cruising at 30mph down the parkway [not something recommended by Mercedes, incidentally] to its rock-solid steering at *any* speed, there isn't one piece of shoddy or make-do workmanship in this neat sports-touring machine. Mind you, this is no racing car – though it could probably be made into one if the factory were inclined to peel off a few hundred pounds in weight, close up the ratios in the gearbox and stiffen up the springs and shocks. True, 190SLs *have* on occasion distinguished themselves in competition. Macau and the Nassau Islander's races for example, but these are rare instances and the circumstances involved could hardly be considered normal.

No, it's not a racing car but it comes close to being an ideal car for going to and from the races – which is just exactly what we used it for. At least one of those trips was an eleven-hour haul each way and the others ranged from six down to two hours. Further,

As first seen at the 1954 New York show, the 190SL prototype looked a little different, especially around the nose and rear arches. Re-styling was only part of the long delay before production.

The prototype in street-racer trim, with fashionably cut down doors and low-drag aero-screen.

A production car at last; the 190SL at Geneva, 1955.

virtually every sort of weather – springtime in Virginia to a minor hurricane in southern Maryland – was encountered and not once did we get that aching fatigue handed out by more prosaic transportation under similar circumstances . . .

END OF THE BEGINNING

Yes, they liked it. And so, of course, did most of the almost 26,000 others who bought 190SLs up to 1963, but by then it was being seen in a different light. In a way, the 190SL's initial strength was also its only long-running weakness. When it was launched it

bathed in the glory of the 300SL alongside it, and people bought it as much for that association as for anything else. But, of course, with only four cylinders and 2 litres, and virtually as much weight to haul around as the 240bhp race-bred 300, it was a very different car indeed.

It was sporty, for sure, as any low-slung, two-seater convertible is almost bound to be, but it was not a sports car in the true sense; it just was not *quite* quick enough or rebellious enough. In spite of the original option of cut-down doors and an aero screen, it had never made any impact as a racer – had people never expected it to, that would not have mattered a damn, but the early

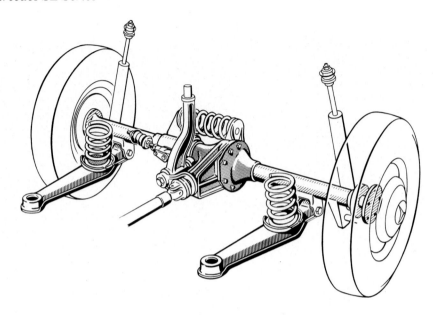

The single-point swing axle with compensating spring was introduced at much the same time on the 220 saloons and the 190SL, and was highly praised for its fine handling.

Simply a good looking little sports car, with the top down . . . or up.

association had been amazingly strong.

Instead, the 190SL drifted towards quite a different image. It was seen as respectable, dripping with quality and even nippy enough for the boulevard cruiser. But by the 1960s, and in the USA in particular which was still the main market, it was a bit staid for the increasingly important young set. For them there were many more racy, yet at the same time more affordable alternatives, not only from the cheaper European stables but now in home-grown product too, especially in the shape of the extremely successful, V8-engined, glass-fibre-bodied Corvette. Ford too had already spotted the new twist to the sporty, youth-oriented market and were about to fill it with the Mustang.

The Mercedes, of course, was never aimed at that catchment anyway, but what had happened was that the wider market had changed, and from being a sports car proper with the racing connotations of the 300s to underline it, the whole SL ethos was shifting. Mercedes were now well and truly back on the high-quality, high-price route and doing very nicely too; the SL tag was still very valuable to them to fulfil the needs of well-heeled customers who wanted to court the sporting fringes but did not want to give up the luxury high ground. The next generation would be designed from the ground up to give them just what they ordered . . .

6 Pagoda Tops and the Second Generation

Depending on how you looked at it, the car with which Mercedes launched the second generation of SLs in 1963 was either the best of both the old worlds or a blatant compromise sitting slightly uneasily between the two.

Since the early 1950s, Mercedes had offered their sports car customers a choice; depending on how fast they wanted to go and how much they wanted to spend, they could choose between the only moderately quick and powerful but temptingly affordable four-cylinder 190SL, or the stunningly fast and impressive but frighteningly expensive six-cylinder 300SLs, in coupé or Roadster form.

Now, the 300, although still the epitome of style, was no longer quick enough to go racing and no longer comfortable or well-equipped enough to be regarded as a real grand tourer; and the 190, always in the 300's shadow, had simply never quite cultivated the glamorous image that buyers expected. Mercedes had had a good run with the first SLs, but even their long-life model cycle eventually had to bow to the fact that they were due for replacement.

The world had moved on since the SLs were launched, and by 1963 the competition was newer and more wide-ranging than ever, particularly with cars like Jaguar's E-Type offering an awful lot of what had made the 300s in particular special, for only a fraction of the price. So Mercedes had to look to what they did best, and offer performance with faultless style and quality. And even they had to face one commercial reality. By the early 1960s, racing sports cars and sporting road cars had become such totally different animals that any possibility of offering both on anything like a common platform was gone; and if that was gone, so too was the possibility of making two different cars profitably.

AN SL FOR ALL TASTES?

The car that Mercedes unveiled at the Geneva Motor Show in mid-March 1963 was a single-model SL range. It was a car conceived as a stylish, comfortable and practical two-seater convertible that, from the start, would have the option of a detachable hard-top, manual or automatic transmissions and other minor running gear options, but only one engine type. Although it was designed under the auspices of the same notoriously sports-minded duo of Nallinger and Uhlenhaut who had conceived the earlier cars, it would not be an out-and-out sports car in the sense of the 300SLs. Instead, it would have enough performance to be amply entertaining, but without the odd shortcomings which had occasionally made the old cars frightening. In fact, it would offer just what the early 1960s Mercedes 'sports car' buyer wanted; the image without the effort.

As the 190SL had borrowed heavily from the 180 parts-bin when it was launched in 1954, so the new car, which was to be called the 230SL, was largely based on the 220SE saloons, but you would hardly have known it just from looking.

The styling verged on the conservative,

The second generation of SLs, coming more than three-quarters of a decade after the first of the breed, was a wholly different kind of car, above and below the skin.

Mercedes emphasized the 'horizontal' styling of the 230SL with the full-width grille, while still managing to evoke the 300SL Roadster with the vertical light units.

but it was instantly recognizable as sporting Mercedes. Even so, it was quite different from any of the SLs that had gone before. Gone was the streamlined, softly rounded look of the older cars, and gone was the implicit aggression of styling features like the side air vents and the aerodynamic wheelarch strakes. You knew this was a different kind of car as soon as you looked at it – a car that was not just a stylish and practical step away from the race-bred first generation but one which did not pretend otherwise.

It was low, wide and much squarer edged; a sharp, closely cut look with maybe a bit too much chrome trim but very little additional ornament, a bit in the mode of the Italian suits that the young smart set wore in the early 1960s. It had vertical headlamp clusters like the 300SL Roadsters, and a clearly recognizable updating of the familiar wide

230SL, 1963–66

Body type	:	two-door, two-seater roadster with folding soft-top and/or detachable hard-top
Chassis	:	platform with unitary body
Engine type	:	in-line six-cylinder
Capacity	:	2,306cc
Bore	:	82.0mm
Stroke	:	72.8mm
Compression ratio	:	9.3:1
Cylinders	:	cast-iron block, seven main bearings
Cylinder head	:	alloy, with two valves per cylinder operated by single, chain-driven, overhead camshaft
Fuel system	:	Bosch indirect mechanical injection
Maximum power	:	170bhp at 5,500rpm
Maximum torque	:	159lb ft at 4,500rpm
Bhp per litre	:	73.7
Gearbox type	:	four-speed epicyclic automatic with fluid coupling
Gear ratios	:	Fourth: 1.10 Second: 2.52
		Third: 1.58 First: 3.98
		Reverse: 4.15
Final drive ratio	:	3.75:1
Clutch	:	n/a
Front suspension	:	unequal-length double wishbones, coil springs, telescopic dampers, anti-roll bar
Rear suspension	:	low-pivot swing axle, longitudinal arms, coil springs plus transverse compensating spring, telescopic dampers
Brakes	:	discs front, drums rear, with servo assistance
Steering	:	recirculating ball with power assistance
Wheels and tyres	:	steel; 185/14in radial-ply tyres
Overall length	:	169.0in (429.3cm)
Overall width	:	69.3in (176.0cm)
Overall height	:	51.4in (130.6cm)
Wheelbase	:	94.5in (240cm)
Track	:	58.0in (147.3cm) front and rear
Ground clearance	:	6.7in (17.0cm)
Fuel tank capacity	:	14.3gal (65 litres)
Unladen weight	:	2,800lb
Power to weight ratio	:	136.0bhp/ton

PERFORMANCE

Maximum speed	:	115mph (185kph)
0–60mph (0–97kph)	:	10.5sec
0–100mph (0–161kph)	:	35.2sec
Standing ¼ mile (0.4km)	:	17.7sec
Fuel consumption	:	approx 18mpg (6.37km per litre)

Even the publicity approach had changed somewhat; no sign of racing drivers now, only swans and calm waters.

grille, but the most distinctive feature of the second generation of SLs was once again in the roof line.

It was not anything quite so dramatic as the gullwings this time, but it was at least enough to earn the model an instant nickname, as the 'pagoda-roof' SL. The epithet suggested itself because the new car's hardtop roof had a very pronounced dip running from front to rear, which obviously gave the road testers something to hang a name on, and the name stuck.

In fact, the roof did not so much have a dip down the middle as two extra-deep portions along the edges, which allowed deeper door openings and side windows, for both better visibility and easier entry and exit. It took five levers to release the hard-top, one behind each sun-visor, two at the back and a final lock in the centre rear, but it was easy

to work and so well fitted that it could have been mistaken for a permanent fixture. It was heavy enough to take two people to lift it off though, and had to be left at home once it was removed; there was obviously no way to stow it on board. The beautifully finished soft-top stowed neatly under a solid cover behind the cockpit. If you chose to, as with the earlier convertible cars, you could take the hard-top without the soft-top for a small discount over choosing both. This liberated slightly more space behind the front seats, but not many SL buyers chose to do this – they naturally preferred the maximum versatility option.

With the hard-top, the 230SL had no less than 38 per cent more glass area than a similarly equipped 190SL, which in its day was considered to be particularly light and airy. In that no one had ever said the

The 230SL was a plainer car altogether than the aggressive looking 300s and even the 190, which had a certain something. Its main visual drama was in its very wide, very low proportioning.

No mistaking where the nickname came from this time; move over gullwings, make way for the pagoda roof.

One thing the pagoda tops did offer, especially in hard-top form, was an exceptional amount of cockpit glass.

The 1963 230SL's single-low-pivot rear suspension (above) and double wishbone front suspension (below), plus the in-line six-cylinder engine with its fuel-injection system.

The reinforced floor frame of the 230 SL is picked out in red. It is welded to the strong body to form one distortion-free unit.

The days of spaceframe chassis were over by the time the 230SL was launched. This is the new car's platform, with welded-on shell and impact absorbing front and rear zones.

This was a car designed from the ground up, starting with new-technology radial tyres with distinctive bumper ribs.

The extremely wide track was designed to take maximum advantage of the new tyres' abilities . . .

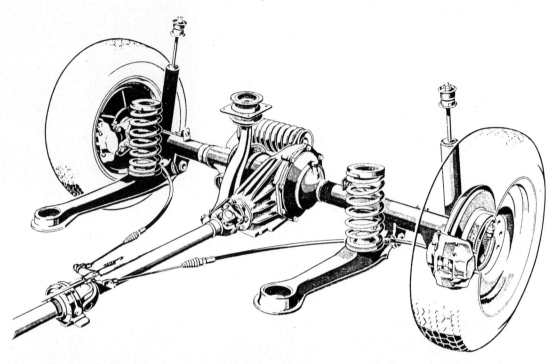

. . . and so was the latest suspension, with flexible rubber mountings, trailing links and compensator spring.

Gullwing was an easy car to get in and out of, the 230 was bound to be an improvement in that respect too. All in all, Mercedes were taking the practicality side of the new 230SL very seriously, while still calling it a sports car. On the road, it turned out to be far more of a sports car than many of the early cynics thought possible . . .

FROM THE GROUND UP

It was no mere re-styling exercise, but a genuinely new car from the ground up. Literally from the ground up, in fact, because one of the things that dictated its wide and low stance was its use of radial tyres and a suspension layout to make the most of them.

Mercedes had learned with the original high-pivot, swing-axle 300SL that all the straight-line performance in the world is wasted if the car either frightens or punishes its driver in corners. Equally importantly, they had learned from the 190SL with its new low-pivot axles that fine handling can go a long way towards making up for relatively meagre power. So Mercedes made design parameter number one for the new SL a quest for exceptional roadholding, yet with the best possible ride comfort. Fortunately for them, that was one of the many things that Rudi Uhlenhaut, with his unrivalled blend of academic skill and hands-on analysis, was brilliantly qualified to produce.

His starting point would be a set of tyres large enough and stable enough to provide adequate grip, but at the same time flexible enough to retain acceptable comfort. These are factors that are taken for granted now, but which were more or less mutually exclusive in the late 1950s and early 1960s when radials were only in their troublesome infancy.

Radial tyres were first developed soon after World War II and patented in mid-1946 by Michelin in France. The original idea was not to provide better grip or handling but principally to provide more acceptable wear, especially on popular French front-drive cars such as the various Citroëns.

Tyres produce their cornering force by running misaligned to push the vehicle laterally round the corner; Michelin's pioneering principle was to reduce the degree of misalignment (or slip angle) needed to produce a particular cornering force, and if the slip angle was reduced then the rate of wear should be too.

Michelin achieved that by creating a very rigid tread, stabilized by an inner band of layers of steel cords acting like a rigid hoop. The foundation was built below from radial cords of rayon, running through the casing from edge to edge, like a continuous arch around the circumference of the wheel. The well-controlled, steel-braced tread gave the tyre its wear resistance, and the flexibility of the construction kept it comfortable.

Michelin launched such a tyre for use on cars as the Michelin X, and it started to become popular in the early to mid-1950s, especially in France. It did what had first been intended, in so far as it could deliver as much as double the mileage expected from a normal cross-ply tyre on a small family car, but it showed other properties too – some good and some not so good. Very basically, early radials with their well-controlled treads and deliberately minimized slip angles produced excellent high-speed ride comfort and especially offered a great deal of cornering power (plus good braking and traction). Unfortunately, however, this was at the expense of low-speed harshness, properly consistent steering response and, worst of all, any worthwhile warning of the onset of final loss of grip.

In the early days drivers of quicker cars who fitted the new radials purely for their cornering power occasionally discovered the lack of feedback the hard way, and none more so than those who fitted them to 300SLs. This was because the combination of radial tyre and high-pivot swing axle was about as nervous as could be; in fact many 300SLs fitted with early Michelin X radials carried a small sticker on the dashboard advising the driver not to exceed 120mph (193kph).

As the 1950s progressed, however, the car makers started to fulfil their side of the equation, and designed suspensions that made better and more predictable use of the desirable qualities of radial tyres and minimized the undesirable ones. Having found suitable ways to get round the Michelin patents, other tyre manufacturers soon began to offer their variations on the radial theme, which were later to include developments like wider treads and lower profiles, and designs steadily progressed.

MADE TO MEASURE

The best radial features were essential to Uhlenhaut's thinking for the new SL, but no tyre existed with all the features he wanted, so Mercedes went to both Firestone and Continental in Germany to have such a tyre made to order.

In a true radial (which has the carcass cords at 90 degrees to the wheel rim) the comfort-giving flexibility of the walls creates an undesirable delay in response between the tread and the rim, and tractive and braking forces also adversely affect steering response. Both Firestone's and Continental's answers to Uhlenhaut's brief were tyres that were essentially radials with their circumferentially-braced treads, but in which the cords ran at an angle from bead to bead, rather than absolutely square. The angle was small, but enough to reduce significantly the

When Mercedes offered the soft-top option, they offered the neatest possible installation, with the lowered hood hidden completely away under a solid metal cover.

The dashboard of the 230SL was instantly recognizable as Mercedes, with its odd steering wheel, its mixture of round and rectangular instruments and just a touch of wood.

The new SLs had grown one stage more luxurious, and the emphasis was now more strongly on comfort than on race car connections.

The 230SL had lost some 14in (36cm) from the related saloon's wheelbase, yet still managed to keep a huge amount of space and accessibility for two occupants.

With such a big greenhouse, ventilation was a priority.

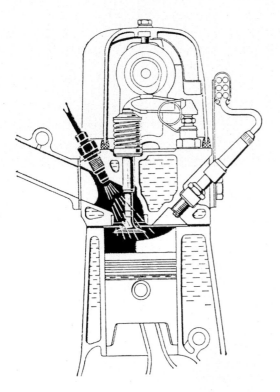

The six-cylinder engines were derived from the 220 saloons and coupés, and by 300 standards maybe they were rather unglamorous. They were better than that, though, and offered a fair balance between refinement and efficiency.

troublesome effects of braking and traction forces, and to minimize the delay in steering response between tread and rim.

Uhlenhaut had also specified a generous tread width and an additional rib on the outer sidewall to resist scuffing on kerbs or stones, conventional radials being very vulnerable to sidewall damage. That was what the new car sat on – with its suspension contrived to take maximum advantage of the new characteristics.

The floorpan and suspension of the 230SL were derived from the 220S and 220SE saloons, and as such included coil springs and telescopic dampers all round. These worked on double wishbones at the front (with an anti-roll bar) and swing axles at the rear, but with a much more refined and forgiving swing-axle layout than the nerve-testing 300SL type.

The 230SL also owed its wide and solid-looking stance to the saloons, in that it kept the same generous track dimensions (58½in (148.6cm) front and rear) while losing a full 14in (35.6cm) out of the wheelbase, to bring the latter down to 94in (239cm) – virtually the same as on both the 300 and 190SLs. Overall, the 230SL was about 6in (15cm) shorter than the 300 and 3½in (9cm) longer than the 190 and although its tracks were about 4in (10cm) and 2in (5cm) wider than the 300's at front and rear respectively, its overall width was around 1in (2.5cm) *narrower*, which contributed to the wide stance look, with the wheels really stretching out the full width into the arches.

The rear swing axle was the single low-pivot type already used on the 190SL and 300SL Roadster, and with the wider track of the 230SL it was better again. In this form it had overcome most of the problems of troublesome camber changes and high roll centre that had made the 300 coupé so tricky at its limits. In the 230SL, the rear layout also had the benefit of the trailing arms as used on the 190SL, and the final refinement was what Mercedes dubbed a 'compensating spring', set horizontally above and between the two axle halves (in effect, across the 'hinge') in such a way as to increase bump resistance but without aggravating load transfer in roll. That allowed Uhlenhaut to achieve the planned effect of comparatively soft springing with firm damping and roll control.

The new SL had Girling disc brakes at the front, but clung to Al-fin drums at the back (plus vacuum servo assistance as standard), and it had the old favourite Mercedes recirculating-ball steering, with a typically over-large wheel dominating the well-trimmed cockpit.

At the car's launch, *Sports Car Graphic* remarked:

The body itself is beautifully finished all

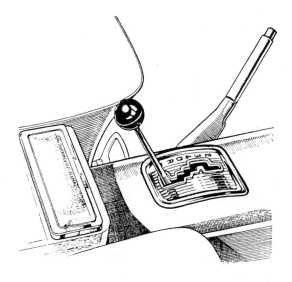

Another sign of the changing character of the SL was the automatic transmission – albeit a highly-praised one.

around and the luxurious, tasteful interior is of the very highest quality. The well-conceived dashboard is very elegant and all instruments are concentrated in a clear, compact unit, which features, of course, a rev counter. Lovely glove quality leather is used to cover the dashboard and trimmings, while, if wanted, the large comfortable bucket type seats can also be had in leather. These seats are fully adjustable (reclining type) and the driver finds an excellent driving position right away. The floor-type stick shift (which is of a similar type in the automatic version) is well-placed, quick and pleasant to use. The hand brake, however, which is located against the gear box tunnel, has a rather crude appearance which contrasts with the general plush appearance of the rest of the car. Another feature which I noticed (although many did not seem to mind this at all) was the rather large steering wheel, which in my opinion, took too much room and could even be an inconvenience for a tall person driving close to it. The car is strictly a two-seater, but a child could find enough space to sit crossways behind

the front seat. The trunk is wide and spacious, certainly enough to please two travellers . . .

Looking at the 230SL now, you certainly could not argue about the quality and the luxury, or even the control layout which reflected the fact that the SL was a car designed by drivers for drivers. The column stalk, for instance, was one of the first multi-function stalks ever offered, and it had most of the features you could expect today. The dashboard, on the other hand, looks very quaint by modern standards, with an awful lot of chrome trim and the odd mixture of two big dials flanking a vertical column of minor gauges. Even on right-hand drive cars, the handbrake lever was always on the left-hand side of the transmission tunnel, which was odd, but not too awkward.

The notional child behind the front seats could have had the option of a third transverse 'occasional seat' (as also offered on the 190SL). If you deleted the soft-top option and took the car with just the removable hard-top, there was even room for something like a bench seat, with a padded backrest, but unfortunately no suggestion as to where one's legs might fit in . . .

BORROWED POWER

The engine hailed from the 220 saloons and coupé (and thus dated back to the 1950s). It had been designed to give ample power for a fairly big and heavy car, but from a capacity small enough not to attract the tax penalties applied to bigger engines in some Mercedes markets. In typical Mercedes style, it was a superbly engineered engine which offered scope for quite high specific output and almost unbreakable ruggedness. It would transfer to the new SL with just enough modification to give it an appropriately more sporting flavour, but still far from enough zest for some tastes.

It was an all-alloy, in-line six-cylinder, with big bore and short stroke, which is a notably excellent layout for refinement and with which Mercedes had had plenty of experience, but it was a rather more conven- tional engine than the one in the 300SLs. The top of the block was flat rather than inclined, the tops of the pistons were flat and the plugs, combustion chambers and fuel injector nozzles were all in the cylinder

Perhaps the strongest styling continuity was in the headlight clusters and the strong horizontal bar through the grille – it was not in the slab sides and square edges.

By earlier standards the rear of the 230SL could only be called fussy, yet it still looks less dated than most contemporaries.

head. The engine was also mounted vertically in the chassis rather than inclined. Its chain-driven single overhead camshaft and adjustable finger rockers operated two valves per cylinder.

In the 220s, this M127 engine had already been widely praised as being exceptionally willing for quite a modest size, especially in terms of low-down flexibility, and for being very smooth and very reliable – even though it only had a four-bearing crankshaft, to balance bottom-end strength with the ability to rev freely. It was not a sporting engine in the manner of the 300SLs, but it is worth remembering that Mercedes took first,

second and third places in the 1960 Monte Carlo Rally with a works team of 220SE saloons. The cars started from Warsaw and were driven by Walter Schock / Rolf Moll, Eugen Bohringer / Hermann Socher and Roland Ott/Eberhard Mahle. A privately entered Dutch 220SE, also starting from Warsaw finished fifth.

For the 230SL, the capacity was increased slightly from the saloon's 2,195cc by increasing the bore by 2mm to give bore and stroke dimensions of 82.0 × 72.8mm and 2,306cc – hence the 230SL designation. The compression ratio was raised from 8.7:1 to 9.3:1, bigger valves, a better exhaust manifold and

The 170bhp 2.3-litre fuel-injected six-cylinder engine.

a more sporty camshaft were specified, and a different type of fuel injection was used.

On the 220SE (for *Sport Einspritz*) Mercedes had used a cheaper and less complex Bosch mechanical injection system than the direct type used on the 300SLs. Instead of the 300SL's six-plunger pump driven at half engine speed and the nozzles injecting directly into the cylinders, the SE installation used a simpler two-plunger pump, operating at engine speed and injecting via six calibrated, fixed nozzles in the air intake side. In this case there was a large, single air-collection plenum with the single throttle body at its forward end, 300SL style, and six individual straight pipes feeding air to the inlet ports. The injector nozzles were in the inlet pipes, just outboard of the cylinder head, so it was an indirect type. For the 230SL, the layout reverted to a six-plunger pump driven at half engine speed, but with the injector nozzles in the head, spraying into the inlet ports towards the back of the valves.

In the 220SE, power output had been quoted at 134bhp at 5,000rpm, and peak torque as 152lb ft at 4,100rpm; in 230SL guise, those figures (in the usual SAE terms – the Society of Automotive Engineers of America figures being gross figures, with engine ancillaries. removed, whereas the DIN figure more normally quoted in Europe are Deutsche Industrie Norme net figures, complete with ancillaries and therefore usually numerically lower) improved to 170bhp at 5,600rpm (or about 150bhp net) and 159lb ft of torque at 4,500rpm. In other words the engine had gained some power but had not done quite so well for flexibility, and although that should have been offset by slightly less weight and more appropriate gearing, it never wholly was.

The transmission options for the 230SL were again 220-derived, and offered either four-speed, all-synchromesh manual or four-speed automatic with epicyclic gear train and fluid coupling – the latter with a notably neat floor-mounted selector and the facility to hold gears manually in the modern manner. Sports car or no, Mercedes expected to supply the large majority of 230SLs with the automatic option. Power-assisted steering was also offered with the automatic transmission, and several early testers, no doubt feeling the grip of the bespoke, 185 × 14in radial tyres on their bolt-on steel wheels, commented that they would have preferred to have the power steering in combination with the manual gearbox, too.

WELL RECEIVED

Sports Car Graphic were as impressed when first driving the car as they had been by looking it over:

When at the wheel of the 230SL for the first time, one is immediately impressed by the sensation of comfort, luxury and outstanding visibility about you. The convenient instruments are easy to read, the turning signal, wipers, washers and lights are all concentrated into one stick gadget on the steering column, easy to use once accustomed to it. The gearbox is quick to respond and the engine, although not entirely dead quiet at maximum revs, is very smooth. It is so smooth and flexible, in fact, that you can actually drive to under 10mph in top gear without making the

engine suffer, and then accelerate away briskly. This is a very good point for a car conceived for high speed touring, and thus for a sport minded clientele.

On the other hand Mercedes has cleverly scored in another way because the type of, let's say, rich-older people buying a Mercedes sports car (previously buying the 190 and 300SL) are not particularly the type who like to do a lot of shifting and thus will undoubtedly greatly appreciate the outstanding flexibility of the 230SL engine. This excellent feature has not, however, prevented Mercedes, who rightly forecast that the clientele for this car will be quite varied, from offering their own automatic transmission as well, which has three forward driving positions and which is handily commanded by a floor shift. I tried it and liked it very much, even for fast driving, and this in spite of a less favourable gear ratio. While mentioning gear ratios, those of the regular four-speed box are good, with first going to 30mph, second to 57, and third to 88mph, this last gear being the only one which could be improved by raising it to, let's say, 95mph or even 100 . . .

THE UHLENHAUT SHOW

If the new 230SL impressed on first aquaintance on the road, that was only part of the story. Although Mercedes were no longer quite so emphatic about the SLs being sports cars *per se*, and certainly were not talking about the 230SL as a car that would double up as a weekend racer (even though it did have a works competition future), they were happy enough to let selected journalists loose on a race-track with assorted variants at the time of the launch, and they seem to have disappointed none of them.

The track was a small but interesting one just across the French border from Geneva, at Montroux (Switzerland would still have nothing to do with motor sports after the 1955 Le Mans accident) and although it was barely three-quarters of a mile long it featured seven widely differing and apparently very revealing bends. As with the first British demonstration of the 300SL coupé at Silverstone back in 1954, Uhlenhaut was on hand to show exactly what the car was capable of, and certainly no one knew better than he.

Among the lucky few who sat in an SL passenger seat while Uhlenhaut showed his genius, was *Autocar*'s correspondent, who reported:

It was in its roadholding that the 230SL was most impressive. Those who maintain that a swing axle rear suspension must produce oversteer should first try this car. Undoubtedly the very wide track of 4ft 10.5in (incidentally 0.5in wider than that of the Jaguar Mk10) contributes to its neutral steering characteristics, but the somewhat expensive single-joint low-pivot point and compensating spring are additional refinements.

A new design of tyre, the *Halbgurtel*, made by Continental, has been developed for this car. It is a braced-tread type with four circumferential rayon bracings, but instead of the wall cords being truly radial they are angled at 10 degrees. Development work on these tyres was instigated in the Daimler-Benz experimental department, and it is claimed that this design possesses the acknowledged advantages of the rigid-breaker tyre adhesion, but overcomes the small degree of lateral instability associated with true radial cords. To see Uhlenhaut cornering under power, with the outer front tyre seemingly being torn away from the rim, made it impossible to question the claims made for this new tyre and no change of attitude between power-on and power-off in corners could be detected.

As we arrived at the Montroux circuit, Michael Parkes, who was responsible for the small Rootes rear-engined car to be announced shortly [a reference to the Hillman Imp], and is now on the engineering staff at

Ferrari, was leaving with a 250GT Berlinetta. We learned that he had lapped the difficult circuit in 47.3sec compared with Uhlenhaut's best of 47.5sec!

Now just to put that into perspective, the 3-litre 1963 250GT would have produced some 240bhp in a car weighing somewhat less than the 2,670lb (1,211kg) Mercedes; and Mike Parkes was not only a highly respected development engineer but a racing driver who had finished second for Ferrari at Le Mans in 1961, who since January 1963 had been in charge of the experimental department at Ferrari (working on both racing and road cars), and who went on to score many championship points in Ferrari's GP cars. In many ways, he was at that time Ferrari's equivalent of Uhlenhaut; the big difference was that Uhlenhaut was not actually allowed to race.

NO MORE TREACHERY

So as not to understate the role of the car in running the Ferrari so close that day, Gordon Wilkins, a journalist of considerable driving skill and vast Mercedes experience, himself managed to lap the 230SL (and this on very first acquaintance with both car and circuit remember) in around 49 seconds. Nor could he catch it out deliberately:

I tried changing course in a corner. No problem. I shut the throttle abruptly in the middle of a full power four-wheel drift. The car slowed down but continued on course.

So next I tried tramping on the brakes right in the middle of a corner while going as fast as I knew how. The car should have spun off. It held right on course. These were no 100mph bends, but on the available evidence I am tempted to rate this as just about the most forgiving fast car I have ever driven. Yet it is quiet and docile with all home comforts, perfectly suitable for a dinner date on a wet winter's night . . .

Away from the test track, the 230SL was reckoned good for a top speed of some 125mph (201kph) or a very few less in automatic form – and acceleration from 0–60mph (0–97kph) in around 9.5 seconds and 0–100 (0–161kph) in about 26.5 seconds. Again, it was marginally slower with the automatic, but the only place the automatic really suffered in acceleration was in getting off the mark; in the higher ranges an automatic car could actually be marginally *quicker* than a manual, according to many testers.

That was partly a corollary of the SL's typically Germanic manual gearing, as inherited from the saloons, with a very low first gear to get the weight on the move, a high top gear commensurate with autobahn cruising, and thus two rather widely spaced ratios in between. Combined with an engine that needed to be worked hard to give of its best, it did invite some criticism.

Even so, the 230SL was launched to almost universal acclaim, with a price in the USA (where most would go) quoted as 'about $5,000', or close to £4,000 in the UK by 1965 with automatic transmission and power steering.

Even at that sort of level (which was almost exactly double the price of a 4.2-litre E-Type in 1965 and not very far behind an Aston DB5), it had been extremely well received. Between 1963 and early 1967, Mercedes sold over 19,800 examples of the 230SL, and sold them at a profit.

They had changed virtually nothing on the car (except to offer different final-drive ratios late in 1965) and the majority of commentators still remained deeply impressed by it – especially by its remarkable chassis. If they had a recurrent criticism at all, it was that the car could use some more power, and especially some more low-down flexibility as an alternative to using the revs and the gearbox to add sparkle. So long as you were prepared to work it hard, the 2.3-litre six was acceptably willing, but you sometimes needed to convince yourself that

it sounded it; *Motor* remarked that when working the car hard enough to give optimum performance, the engine sounded busy enough to make you either 'wince or beam', and that, of course, was at odds with the image of entertainment without effort.

BIGGER AND BETTER

In March 1965, again at the Geneva show, the SL got what the critics had been asking for, thanks to a marginally bigger and usefully more torquey engine. It was not just a straight upgrade of the 2.3-litre unit, but a new and stronger engine with seven-main-bearing crankshaft based on the one introduced in the 250 series saloons at the Frankfurt Motor Show in August 1965. The basic layout was the same, with single, chain-driven overhead camshaft and two-valves per cylinder, and the bore stayed the same at 82.0mm, while the stroke was lengthened by 6.2mm, to 79.0mm, for a capacity of 2,496cc. With a compression ratio of 9.5:1, and a revised cylinder head with bigger valves and ports, and much the same fuel-injection system, maximum power was unchanged, with 170bhp at 5,600rpm, but the torque peak was improved by almost ten per cent at the same engine speed as before, to 174lb ft at 4,500rpm, and both power and torque had been given a more even spread.

Mercedes still offered the option of four-speed manual or four-speed auto, and left internal ratios as on the old car, but now with a slightly taller final drive ratio for the manual option. That was intended to make the most of the improved torque by making the car slightly less frenetic to drive quickly. That meant the maximum speed had gone up only very slightly, while the driver could either convert the better torque spread into marginally sharper acceleration or return the old car's figures with rather less audible drama.

Car & Driver loved virtually everything about the car but were not totally convinced by the gearing:

One feature of the drive train we did object to was the choice of rear axle ratio. The 3.92 ratio that comes with the automatic is too high. With only 18.7mph per 1,000rpm, you're turning 3,200 at 60, and 5,350 at 100mph. It's a tribute to the sound deadening of the car that 100mph cruising speeds aren't particularly fatiguing, but your ears are conscious of an electric motor-like humming from the engine compartment. At the expense of some mid range acceleration, you can get a 3.58 ratio with the manual four-speed . . .

There was also now the option of a ZF five-speed manual gearbox, which should obviously have given better spacing of the intermediate ratios because there was one more of them, and in so far as fifth was an overdrive ratio, it made for more relaxed high-speed progress. The fact is, though, that it was of very little interest to the typical 250SL customer, not just because, as *Car & Driver* commented, 'it takes forever to get and costs an extra $464', but because the said driver was generally more inclined to take the automatic anyway – around half of them did.

Visually, the only thing that had changed was the badge on the boot (to 250SL of course), but also in line with the 250SE saloon, the SL was given disc brakes at the back as well as at the front. To avoid any danger of the rear wheels locking prematurely, a new pressure balancing valve was fitted. The fuel tank capacity was increased slightly in case the extra engine capacity damaged the not especially impressive cruising range, and some extra oil cooling was added.

THE FINAL UPGRADE

For once this proved to be a remarkably

short-lived model, and survived for rather less than a year before Mercedes gave it a final updating that would see this second SL generation through to the end of its production life. In that time they sold just short of 5,200 examples of the 250SL, making it the rarest of the 'pagoda roofs' and perhaps a frustrating mistake for those buyers who, with hindsight, might have waited a few more months for the 280. However, it was still a considerable success in that Mercedes' total annual output around this time was only in the region of 200,000 cars a year.

Once again, the upgrading seems pretty minor on paper for a car that was already five years into production and was presumably intended to survive for a while longer yet, but that is the Mercedes way. This time, the M130 engine had its bore centres moved slightly further apart in order to accommodate a 4.5mm bore increase, from the long-serving 82.0mm to 86.5mm. The stroke was left at 78.8mm so the capacity had edged up to 2,778cc. The compression ratio was left alone, at 9.5:1 and otherwise the engine was pretty much the same as the 250 version. In spite of the bigger capacity it was also generally regarded as being just as free-revving and responsive as the smaller engines.

By the time it appeared in 1968 there was the added complication of different specifications for different markets (notably America) to contend with, so there were minor variations between engines for domestic and export markets. This time, both power and torque had been improved, and for the German enthusiast market the engine supposedly gave as much as 195bhp at 5,900rpm, but everyone else had to be content with rather less.

For America, where emissions were becoming a dirty word, the 2.8-litre engine used less valve overlap, slightly revised fuel injection calibration, and a fuel shut off on deceleration at anything under 1,500rpm. Nevertheless, the generous American SAE figures (that is with engine shorn of ancillaries)

Unusually for a Mercedes, Pininfarina tried a styling exercise on the pagoda-topped SL, but aside from the grille would you really know it was a Mercedes?

now read 180bhp at 5,700rpm (up from 170bhp at 5,600rpm) and 193lb ft of torque at 4,500rpm (from 174lb ft at the same revs); in European terms the normal quote was 170bhp at 5,750rpm and 177lb ft at 4,500rpm.

Again, such other changes as there were were hidden behind a steadfastly unchanging face, although there were in fact several of them, and they had a significant effect on the character of the car. Mostly, they were in deference to new US Federal safety and environmental regulations, and most had already been seen on very late examples of the short-lived 250SL. There were improved, three-point-mounting seat belts, and an energy absorbing steering column with a safer design of steering wheel centre (though with just as big a rim). The handles for unlatching the hard- and soft-tops from the front header rail (which had previously been fixed, and rather nasty for anyone making contact with them in an accident) were made removable and provided with a small stowage bag. Indicator repeaters were added on the front and rear wings. Internal lighting was improved too, to reduce the 'fumble-factor'

with useful night-time illumination for the automatic gearshift gate and clearer lights on the heater and ventilator controls.

Such detail improvements were all suitably appreciated and the 280SL received the same sort of enthusiastic welcome that had been normal throughout the SL's career. *Road & Track*, for instance, reckoned in August 1968:

Some cars don't change, they just get better. The Mercedes-Benz 280SL, latest version of a line that began as the 230SL in 1963, is the same as ever, just better. We always felt the 230SL was a great car but very short on torque and rather fussy in its performance. When the 250SL came along in 1967 the extra displacement gave a worthwhile boost in torque and the seven-bearing crankshaft meant a smoother, quieter engine; all round disc brakes replaced the 230SL's disc/drum system at that time too. Now, with the 280SL, there's another good boost in torque plus a few minor changes, most of which are connected with safety and emissions laws . . .

A SLIGHT CHANGE OF TONE

They went on to praise the new engine, and as everyone did they lauded the handling, brakes, ride and especially the power-assisted steering of the SL but, unmistakably, a new note of qualification was creeping in:

Handling is near neutral, with quick response to any steering input; but the single-pivot swing axles at the rear don't give quite the adhesion that a more up-to-date system would, so that it's easy to tweak out the rear end. The big, sticky Firestone Phoenix radial tires give fairly high cornering limits, but it's obvious that the added torque of the 280 engine brings this venerable suspension close to the end of its usefulness . . .

That stopped short of mentioning the fact that in improving the servicing intervals of the SL from the 230's ridiculously short 2,000-mile (3,219km) greasing intervals to a more acceptable 6,000 miles (9,656km) on the 280, the suspension had latterly gained a lot more rubber bushing, which had taken away some of the old precision and made the car feel less sharp in its control response. The tyres had changed too from the original, very special, low-angle bias-corded covers, to something more nearly like a totally conventional radial, with near 90 degrees cord angles – to avoid some undesirable internal side-effects of the special construction at higher speeds. They had stayed at the same size though, throughout the life of this SL generation, and what had looked extremely generous in 1963 was starting to look a bit mean heading towards 1970.

So were some of the 280SL's other features, especially in view of the fact that Mercedes' latest saloons suddenly had several develop

(Opposite) The lines of the 230SL with its 'pagoda' hard-top in place were simple yet distinctive and elegant.

ments well in advance of the sports car. As *Road & Track* concluded even in 1968:

The 280SL is a complex car, especially in the engine compartment with the mechanical fuel injection system looking like a graduate project at the Institute of Plumbing Engineers. But it is a well-proven, reliable car and the quality of its execution is a delight to the connoisseur of fine automotive machinery. It is somewhat paradoxical that this car does not offer the latest engineering developments of Mercedes-Benz – the improved automatic transmission, the anti-dive front suspension or the new semi-trailing rear suspension – but these probably won't be forthcoming for at least a year . . .

In fact it would be rather more than a year, and then the new features would appear on a wholly new car, not on the faithful old 280. The ones that the magazine had been alluding to included a new four-speed automatic gearbox which not only had better ratios but which also used all four gears from a standstill, where the old one left the line in second unless you gave it a violent kick-down. Then there was modern anti-dive geometry for the front wishbone suspension (and it is remarkable, reading back, how many testers latterly criticized the SL for pronounced nose dive under heavy braking), and an all-new, semi-trailing-link rear suspension layout which was clearly better than even the best of the swing axles.

In the meantime, late in 1970, *Autocar*, while admitting that at the top end of the two-seater market the 280SL still had barely a single rival in the world, had time to say roughly the same as everyone else: 'At just over £5,000 it is far from cheap, and in a few ways it is beginning to show the age of the original concept . . .'

Mercedes, fortunately, had already figured that out quite some time ago, and a spectacularly new SL, with all the modern features that anyone could ask for, plus a return to power, was only a matter of months away.

7 SLs for a Changing World

By the late 1960s, Mercedes and the SL family had a problem. In many of the SL's most important markets, it was starting to be considered irresponsible even to mention the term 'sports car'. Worst of all, the strongest reaction was right in the SL's marketing heartland – America.

As the environmental and safety lobbies became more vociferous and influential, the outlook for many motor manufacturers was changing dramatically, especially if, say, they happened to make conspicuously consumptive, high performance soft-tops. As early as the mid-1960s, Mercedes had recognized the trend and concluded that they were faced with only two options for the SL concept: they must either change it to make it less antagonistic to the protectionists, or scrap it altogether.

Happily for SL enthusiasts, the sales figures, prestige value and profitability for the models in the 'sports car' line were still such that Mercedes was not about to sign it off yet, so 'all change', it would have to be.

That would fit in quite acceptably with their overall policy of making increased profits without having to build very many more cars. In world terms Mercedes, for all their prestige, really ranked only as a medium-sized manufacturer, and as such their ability to expand by expanding production volume was strictly limited. The alternative was to sell not many more cars but sell them with the added value items of luxury and style piled on, and prices and profitability increasing in parallel.

That was not even a possibility for manufacturers with a lesser reputation, but at the Mercedes end of the market, flagship cars – cars which sold on image – traditionally were not overly sensitive to price, and image was exactly what had been selling the SL for many, many years.

A FRESH START

What is more, it was still selling them in very attractive numbers, with production holding steady at something near the 6,000 units a year mark. That was not a lot of cars in true mass-production terms, but as well as being sold profitably, they could also be reasonably regarded as 6,000 rolling advertisements for lesser models. The equation was made doubly acceptable to the Stuttgart bean counters in so far as they were only very occasionally asked to send funds in the other direction for changes or updates.

Now, however, they needed to invest in the future, and in this case they had to invest in rather more than just another minor updating. As before, the SL would be offered with a soft-top, a removable hard-top or both, but by the time this third generation appeared, in the middle of 1971, about the only other thing it had in common with its predecessors was four wheels, two seats and the SL badge. As for the latter, Mercedes still maintained that the initials stood for *Sport Licht*.

More than with any of the two-seater line to date, though, their marketing emphasis was shifting inexorably away from overtly

350SL 4.5 (US specification), 1971–80

Body type	:	two-door, two-seater roadster with folding soft-top and/or detachable hard-top
Chassis	:	platform with unitary body
Engine type	:	90° V8
Capacity	:	4,520cc
Bore	:	91.9mm
Stroke	:	85.1mm
Compression ratio	:	8.0:1
Cylinders	:	cast-iron block, five main bearings
Cylinder heads	:	alloy, with two valves per cylinder operated by single, chain-driven, overhead camshaft per cylinder bank
Fuel system	:	Bosch electronic injection
Maximum power	:	230bhp at 5,000rpm
Maximum torque	:	279lb ft at 3,200rpm
Bhp per litre	:	50.9
Gearbox type	:	three-speed epicyclic automatic with torque converter
Gear ratios	:	Third: 1.00 First: 2.31 Second: 1.46 Reverse: n/a
Final drive ratio	:	3.07:1
Clutch	:	n/a
Front suspension	:	unequal-length double wishbones, coil springs, telescopic dampers, anti-roll bar
Rear suspension	:	semi-trailing arms, coil springs, telescopic dampers, anti-roll bar
Brakes	:	ventilated discs front, solid discs rear, with servo assistance
Steering	:	recirculating ball, with power assistance
Wheels and tyres	:	steel (alloy optional); 205/70VR14 radial-ply tyres
Overall length	:	172.1in (437.1cm)
Overall width	:	70.5in (179.1cm)
Overall height	:	51.2in (130.0cm)
Wheelbase	:	96.9in (246.1cm)
Track	:	57.2in (145.3cm) front, 56.7in (144.0cm) rear
Ground clearance	:	6.5in (16.5cm)
Fuel tank capacity	:	23.8USgal (90.1 litres)
Unladen weight	:	3,670lb (1,665kg)
Power to weight ratio	:	140.4bhp/ton

PERFORMANCE

Maximum speed	:	125mph (201kph)
0–60mph (0–97kph)	:	10.5sec
0–100mph (0–161kph)	:	29.5sec
Standing ¼ mile (0.4km)	:	17.9sec
Fuel consumption	:	approx 13mpUSg (5.5km per litre)

Still a sports car? The third generation of SLs had come a long way since the race-car-derived gullwings, but within the refinement there was still some of the SL spirit in cars like the 350SL

Investing in the future; in the face of the world's new sensitivity to environmental problems, engines had to get cleaner – even if, as in the case of the new 3.5-litre V8, they had to grow bigger and less efficient first.

sporty motoring and towards luxury and safety. By the time this car appeared, both the sports and the lightweight designations would be highly questionable. That was the path down which design was being pushed; already Mercedes (and indeed most other manufacturers) were starting to have a lot less say in the matter and the legislators were starting to have rather more – especially in the USA, which was where most SLs could be expected to go.

So when Mercedes accepted that the SL must change mechanically, they knew it had to change philosophically too. New and pending US Federal regulations meant that all types of cars were about to become stronger, safer and less polluting even if, ironically, that meant that first they had to go through a phase of becoming bigger, heavier and less efficient. In fact, it seems that during its development period, the new SL was affectionately known within the engineering fraternity as *der Panzerwagen*, in an only half-joking reference to the weight of the well-known tank.

For this generation, the choice for Mercedes (once they had accepted that the SL name would survive) had been between total re-engineering within the old shell, or total re-engineering with a new shell; or in other words, no choice at all. The third generation SLs would be all new, very luxurious, very high priced and very socially acceptable.

For the final time, the old hierarchy was in charge of the new project, headed by Rudi Uhlenhaut, even though his retirement was now looming. Mercedes' Engineer-in-Chief was now Dr Ing Hans Scherenberg, who had been responsible for much of the racing car design in the Uhlenhaut era, including, of course, a major role in the W196 GP programme and the successful spin-off of the 300SLR sports racing cars.

Such men love nothing more than the chance to start with a clean sheet of paper; with the new SLs they could answer all those criticisms handsomely that were starting to sneak into the later tests of the 280SL family – criticisms about the ill-matched automatic transmissions and engines that needed to be worked tiresomely hard, the now dated rear suspension, the over-sensitive brakes and the lack of modern anti-dive front suspension geometry. Nor could you help but notice that such criticisms were made all the more frustrating to their authors by the fact that most of the remedies they craved were already to be seen in the newer generations of Mercedes saloons, and apparently only needed transplanting into the SL.

ANSWERING THE CRITICS

When the new car appeared, it would have more power, all-new suspension, superb brakes and the sort of transmissions that the critics ordered, but first of all it would have a new look, so that even the non-technical would understand that it was more than just a face-lift.

The styling process for the new model, designated W107 in factory-speak, stretched over approximately four years. It was dominated by the familiar problems of designing a car that would be recognizably Mercedes, recognizably SL and that could be expected to look fresh for many years to come.

The basic shape began to set quite early, and was certainly evident by 1968. It was especially apparent in the hard-top roof line, which retained a hint of the pagoda profile but which also had a distinctively different, upswept rear side window line, even if the boot lid was eventually given a mild degree of concavity to echo the pagoda roof theme.

The main body line now had a mild but noticeable wedge profile, such as was being popularized by most racing cars at the time and which was *de rigueur* for any manufacturer who wanted to appear in touch with the times. Those cars which exaggerated the wedge shape (and there were plenty of them) quickly started to look corny, but Mercedes treated it with characteristic subtlety and it aged graciously . . .

Some of the early W107 drawings, on the other hand, look uncharacteristically over-adorned for a car that was eventually expected to bear the three-pointed star. They were especially gaudy around the tail, where several renderings showed some very strange, straked vents just ahead of the rear lights on the sides of the body. In some cases those were in addition to a version of the old vents in the front wings, which Mercedes were obviously tempted to use as a reminder of the earliest SLs.

When the final styling was completed though, conservatism had prevailed, and the third generation SLs were as stylish and understated as could be, yet with that unmistakable Mercedes aura of solid quality.

They were bigger pretty well all round than their immediate predecessors. They were almost 2½in (6.5cm) longer in the wheelbase than the 280SL, giving a bit more space behind the seats for children or luggage, and some ahead of the cockpit for new air-conditioning equipment, which was now built in rather than added on. They were more than 3in (7.5cm) longer overall and fractionally wider. The only major dimension that had come down was the height, to give the SL a longer, wider, lower look than ever before.

That did take a bit of help from the stylists, especially in disguising the rather large and flat flanks between the wheelarches; they did it by adding fluted ribs along the lower quarters, below a styling line linking the front and rear bumper levels, as a visual trick to make the car look even longer and lower. They claimed a practical purpose too, in that they supposedly kept spray and road dirt down, away from the side windows.

The front end treatment had changed from perpendicular (with the familiar, tall light clusters) to horizontal, with the wide, rectangular headlights (on European cars at least) continuing into indicator lenses that wrapped right around the corners. Incidentally, these also removed the need for indicator repeater lamps such as later 280s had had to tack on for the American market. At the back, the rear light clusters were given very pronounced ribbing, which not only emphasized the width but also kept the lenses clean by their aerodynamic effect. They immediately became a strong Mercedes styling hallmark.

WEIGHT VERSUS STRENGTH

Inescapably, the other number that had grown quite noticeably was the SL's weight – by as much as 300lb (136kg) when the new car was launched. There was a pressing reason for this: America was introducing new standards on front, rear and side impact protection, and by 1972 there would be tougher rules on engine emissions which demanded heavy control equipment.

So far as body structure was concerned, by 1973 cars offered for sale in the USA would have to be capable of withstanding a 5mph (8kph) frontal collision or a 2½mph (4kph) rear impact without damage to safety-related features such as lights or fuel tank. That was about to manifest itself most notoriously in America in the form of big and invariably hideous 'safety bumpers'. Sometimes, as in the classic example of the MGB, it added up to the complete ruination of the car's looks and even its handling, because the whole body had to be raised on the suspension to bring the nasty new bumpers up to the regulation height.

As the standards became even tougher, so would the body structure itself. But stronger bodies in the early stages of this technology meant yet more weight, and yet more weight meant more energy to dissipate in an impact. This went on *ad infinitum* unless, like Mercedes, the manufacturer was clever enough to make every bit of weight count in effective controlled-deformation structures.

The new SL was conventional enough in that it had a platform chassis with the unitary shell and its internal strengthening structures welded to it to form one strong assembly. Another contribution to the extra weight over that of the 280SL was that for the new car the whole body skin would be of steel, whereas the 280 and kin had used some aluminium panels.

The fuel tank was moved a long way forwards, from under the boot floor to a position above the rear axle and between the rear wheels, for maximum resistance to any rear-end impact. As well as the front and rear impact protection, Mercedes took great care in providing roll-over resistance, just in case any future SL owner should drive the car aggressively enough to invert it. They used new computing power to analyse the complete stresses involved in using the

Although America was becoming increasingly wary about the safety aspect of soft-tops, Mercedes still offered a choice.

The grille, with its big badge and horizontal bar, consciously maintained the familiar SL identity.

Selling the virtues of luxury and style. The seats are non-standard ones in this 350SL, but the increasing emphasis on space and comfort showed.

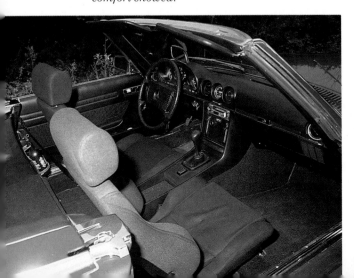

A bigger car, with a mild but noticeable wedge profile and a hard-top roof line to evoke the pagoda tops – the skills of creating a new look but with continuity.

With a couple more inches in the wheelbase, there was room for usefully bigger doors.

Wrap-around treatment for the indicator lenses removed the need for side repeaters in some markets.

The change from perpendicular to horizontal, putting even more emphasis on the low height and width.

steeply raked windscreen pillars as a roll-over bar, while keeping them slim enough for the stylists. They also gave the pillars a profile designed to improve their aerodynamics and act as deflectors to keep water and dirt from the side windows – a typical bit of Mercedes thoroughness, along the lines of the wheelarch strakes on the first 300SL.

Some of the extra width was also forced on the car by the tougher crash requirements. The doors were designed to resist side impacts but without using additional internal reinforcement, which meant that although they were perhaps not quite so heavy as they could have been, they were bulky.

BORROWING THE BEST

Once again, much of the running gear was borrowed from the saloon car line, which in this case was what the critics had been advocating all along, so that was not a problem. The suspension derived from the 250-series saloons (as launched in 1968) and as such was the most advanced in the Mercedes range. At the front it was the latest refinement of the familiar coil-spring and double wishbone layout, with conventional anti-roll bar, but it now also incorporated the anti-dive geometry whose absence from the 280SLs had so often been lamented.

At the rear the suspension had changed much more radically. The low-pivot swing-axle layout was replaced by a semi-trailing arm arrangement, in which the final drive unit was carried by a substantial fabricated subframe which also carried the wide-based forward pivots of the semi-trailing arms. Combined coil-spring/damper units sat between the arms and the bodyshell, and there was an anti-roll bar behind the final-drive and jointed driveshafts. The telescopic dampers had rubber bushes at their top mounts, doubling as bumpstops, and what Mercedes called 'auxilliary springs' when they were on only part compression.

A degree of anti-squat was built in, but not as much as some people would have liked. If enough anti-squat had been built in to stop the car sitting on its haunches any more under power, it would have adversely affected the handling and ride, so for once Mercedes accepted the compromise.

At least this layout finally rid the SL of the notorious swing-axle camber changes – or certainly reduced them by half. Another big improvement was the fact that the new suspension system, being entirely rubber bushed and with sealed ball joints, was 'maintenance-free', where the earlier cars had had such irritatingly short greasing intervals – as short as 2,000 miles (3,219km) on the 230SL.

The wheels and tyres had finally grown a bit, too, though by some standards they were still considered rather modest; normal wear was now 205/70VR14 radials on 6½in wide, bolt-on steel wheels. Europe had the option of some rather attractive alloy wheels, too. Typical tyre choice was Dunlop SPs with Michelin XVRs as a popular option, but the combination of smaller diameter wheels, lower sidewall profiles and the bigger body, somewhat perversely made the new car look positively *under*-tyred compared to the pagoda-top generation.

Like the 250 and 280SL, the 350 had disc brakes all round, but for the first time these used ventilated front discs, inherited from the heavier saloons. The steering (about which there had rarely been any complaints) was again by Mercedes' power-assisted recirculating-ball system; if that had any shortcoming it was the inevitable one of the wheel being too big, which was something that Mercedes, then and now, seemed doggedly resistant to change.

V8 POWER

Most SL buyers, however, were probably

*The pronounced ribbing on the rear light
lenses (as here on an SLC) was functional as
well as stylish, and designed to keep the
lights clean by controlling airflow.*

very little concerned with what was buried
quite so deep below the surface as suspension and steering. So, styling aside, the most
conspicuous change for the new SL was the
move from in-line six to V8 engines for
power, refinement and the ability to meet
new and pending emissions regulations.

The 3.5-litre unit was not designed specifically for the SL, but it was quite a new engine,
inherited from the recently introduced
medium-sized saloons, the 280SE 3.5 and
300SEL 3.5. It was a very modern, if thoroughly conventional unit; an iron-blocked,
alloy-headed 90 degrees V8 with a single
overhead camshaft for each cylinder bank
(driven by chains), and five main bearings.

In 3.5-litre form it was very oversquare,
with a bore of 92.0mm and a stroke of only
65.8mm, which gave it the desirable characteristics of large valve and piston areas and
the ability to rev happily to some 6,500rpm.
The valves were angled quite steeply towards
the centre of the vee, which kept the engine
attractively narrow across the tops of the
cam covers. It was much more of a European
thoroughbred type V8 than an American

style slogger, but so far as America was
concerned, any V8 was better than any six.

It had a capacity of 3,499cc, a compression
ratio of 9.5:1, Bosch electronic fuel injection
(with the throttle body and metering in the
centre of the vee and the injectors upstream of the valves), and transistorized
ignition. It produced 230bhp at 5,800rpm
(SAE, the DIN figure this time was 200) and
a torque peak of 231lb ft (or 211 DIN) at
4,200rpm.

In the saloons the engine had been paired
with a three-speed automatic transmission
with torque convertor, but for the European-
spec SL, Mercedes initially retained the older
four-speed automatic with fluid coupling –
possibly reasoning that the one thing this
car did not need was additional torque mul-
tiplication. There was no manual option,
even for Europe and even if the SL was a
sports car.

MAKING UP THE NUMBERS

The new model was launched in Europe in
mid-1971, as the 350SL. When the first examples arrived in Britain in June, they were
priced at £5,457, or approximately double the
price of the contemporaneous V12 E-Type.
And if Mercedes were promoting the comfort
and style aspects, they were not understating
the performance; they claimed a maximum
speed of around 130mph (209kph) and 0–
60mph (0–97kph) in just under 9 seconds,
which would make the 350SL quicker than
the similarly powered coupé, and quicker
than the 280SL. As if to confirm that they had
not entirely abandoned the sports car ethic,
the 350SL was shown off to the press for the
first time at the Hockenheim circuit in
Germany; and who should be there to
demonstrate it, of course, but Herr Uhlenhaut – armed additionally with one car
which had stiffer suspension settings and
racing tyres for the occasion.

So that was the birth of the new SL generation for Europe, as the 350SL, but the futility of the new puritanism across the Atlantic was shown by the fact that in the USA the car immediately became the 350SL 4.5 when it arrived in August with all certification complete. After all, the emission regulations had been met, the engine size had had to be increased by a full litre, simply to bring it back to where it started in terms of power – and with the additional body weight it certainly could not afford to have less.

This demanded a heavily modified engine, but it had to be done. The problem was that in those fairly early days of serious emissions control, the engineers could modify the ignition timing, compression ratios and mixture strength. They could also bolt on such closed-circuit breathing systems and the like as were available to reduce hydrocarbon, carbon monoxide and oxides of nitrogen emission, but all this was only at the expense of horsepower – and sometimes lots of horsepower. In taking the 3.5-litre V8 from what it had to achieve in 1970 to what it had to manage in 1972, let alone beyond that, they would have ended up with an overweight, underpowered SL that could barely get out of its own way.

In a way, having to make the modifications was not as big a nuisance to Mercedes as it might seem, because being an engine at the start of its useful life, the 3½-litre V8 had had plenty of scope for enlargement built in. Even so, it was more than just a simple bore and stroke job to take the capacity to 4,520cc. The bore was left at the original 92.0mm but the stroke was lengthened from 65.8mm to no less than 85.0mm – a 19.2mm increase, or around 30 per cent. That involved a new crankshaft, naturally, but also a new block with deeper cylinder bores. The heads also had to be changed, with bigger combustion chambers to bring compression down to 8.0:1. The lower compression was needed to counter high emissions of oxides of nitrogen which were the corollary of running combustion temperatures high enough to control carbon monoxide and hydrocarbon emissions.

Milder camshafts were used, with the ignition timing heavily retarded and the mixture run as weak as possible, all of which tended to make the engine notoriously temperamental at low speeds. And it really *was* strangled, to the extent that it had no more power whatsoever than the European 3.5-litre version, just the same 230bhp (SAE) at a slower-revving 5,000rpm; the only way it did improve was in offering a thumping torque increase and at even lower revs, to a mighty 279lb ft peak at only 3,200rpm.

Yet strangely, Mercedes now paired the US 4.5-litre engine with the three-speed-plus-torque-convertor automatic, with no other option. The fact was, they did not have a manual gearbox capable of handling the torque of this version of the engine, and by offering only one option for the US market they would only have to certify one set of fuel and ignition parameters to satisfy the emissions regulations. The fact that the 4.5-litre engine used, even by Mercedes' own admission, some 10 per cent more fuel than the 3.5-litre engine for the same power was just an unfortunate side-effect.

THE LUXURY TOUCH

One thing that Mercedes did manage to do with the slightly bigger SL body was to find a tiny bit more space inside, so that now instead of just being able to carry one child across the back seat space, you could at a pinch squeeze in two, and some token padding was offered as an option. The front seats were anything but token, but heavily shaped and extremely comfortable once the initial firmness had eased.

The SL now offered lap and diagonal inertia-reel seat belts and they drew a good deal of favourable comment. At the time they

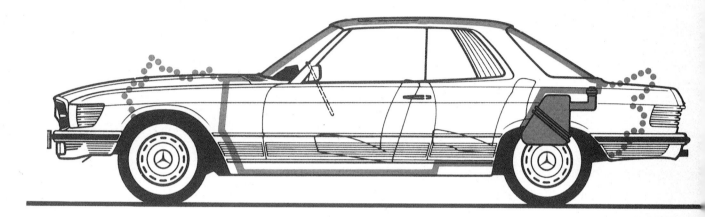

*Even before crash-resistance requirements had been made more stringent,
Mercedes had had a superb reputation for safety. Front and rear crumple zones
(as here on an SLC but virtually identical on the SLs) helped pass barrier
impact tests, and the fuel tank was located for the best protection.*

were a real novelty; as late as 1970, wearing
seat belts was not compulsory anywhere in
the world, although several countries (including Britain) required that they were
fitted on all new cars. The first place to make
the wearing of belts compulsory was the
state of Victoria, Australia, in January
1971, just a few months before the 350SL
was launched. In the USA, compulsory
wearing of seat belts still had not become
universal even by the end of the third generation SLs, let alone at the beginning.

The multi-function steering column stalk
was still noteworthy, remotely adjustable
door mirrors were also a novelty on a European car and there was a rechargeable torch
in the glove box. However, maybe the most
novel feature of all was the fact that the
typically thorough heating and ventilating
system even warmed or cooled the inner
door panels, to complete the luxury touches.

On a more normal level, the dashboard
had been totally redesigned and was now
much less glittery and a lot neater, with
three big main dials in a single pod and with
very legible white-on-black markings. The
control layout showed that Mercedes still
designed for drivers.

Although some testers found the car to be
barely as quick as the 280SL thanks to the
weight and tall gearing, there were few real
complaints, in fact quite the opposite. The
new suspension, in particular, impressed
virtually everybody, including *Road &
Track*, whose first test reported:

It's in the chassis department that the
350SL has the clearest advantage over its
predecessor. At the front, angled A-arms
provide a moderate degree of anti-dive effect
and get rid of the 280SL's severe front-end
squash on braking. More importantly, the
rear swing axles are gone, replaced by semi-
trailing arms which keep rear wheel camber
close to ideal in cornering. As a result, the
350SL is thoroughly up-to-date in handling.

Stronger shells meant more weight and more weight demanded more power —
the SL shell was now all steel.

Its much larger tyres – 70-series radials on 6½in rims – have more weight to cope with but still improve the SL's cornering ability from 0.674g (280SL) to an even 0.700g. That's with Dunlop SPs, which squeal a lot and are rather soft; perhaps the alternate Michelin XVRs would do even better.

The standard power steering, always outstanding, has been further improved and is slightly quicker than before. Its road feel is perfect, for a very simple reason: pull at the steering-wheel rim is absolutely proportional to effort required at the tyres up to the parking-effort level.

Handling is close to neutral, a discreet amount of understeer being present under nearly all conditions to stabilize things. The tail will still come out if the throttle foot is lifted in a hard turn, but it does so gently and controllably and causes no problems. Perhaps the best thing we could say about the SL's handling is that we have absolutely no complaint.

The ride has been improved too. In the old car it was already outstanding, but the new SL is even better at taking monstrous bumps and dips than the old one. No matter what the road surface, you just keep on driving fast and the chassis (not to mention the absolutely stiff, rattle-free body) takes care of you. Amazing. And it's also utterly smooth on good roads too; very little harshness, pitching at a minimum, and so forth. There is no better combination of ride and handling.

Braking is very good too. No Mercedes has exhibited fade in our fade test for years, and the 350SL's ventilated front discs ensure that tradition is continued. The front wheels lock if you keep your foot jammed on in a panic stop, but there is no tendency for the car to get sideways and the driver will never be panicked by the SL's behaviour in an emergency. For everyday driving, the vacuum boost seems to have been tamed somewhat from the 280SL, the pedal no longer being too light for gentle brake applications.

Mercedes' anti-skid braking system will be available shortly after you read this; at this point it hasn't been decided whether to make it standard or optional. When it is available the SL will have the best passenger-car brakes in the world.

In summary, the 350SL is the ultimate in a two-seater luxury car. Its great weight, luxury equipment and mandatory automatic transmission keep it from being a sports car or an entertainment machine, but if one desires merely to drive fast in supreme comfort and avoid the clumsiness of a big sedan, there is no better choice than the 350SL.

As launched in the USA, the price on the east coast was $10,500, which included air conditioning, the three-speed automatic, power steering and brakes, plus the removable hard-top and folding soft-top. Top speed did not quite come up to the 130mph (209kph) claim at 124mph (200kph), and 0–60mph (0–97kph) took 10.5 seconds rather than the claimed sub-9 seconds.

With a litre less, remember, the European car proved a touch quicker than the US one when *Autocar* first tried a 350SL. They managed 126mph (203kph), 0–60mph (0–97kph) in a most respectable 9.3 seconds and 0–100mph (0–161kph) in 26 seconds dead. This car had the four-speed auto, and they did not like it very much, describing it as 'stodgy and unresponsive when left to itself, and except at near full throttle it is reluctant to change down for hills taken at quite low speeds, while the V8 engine is surprisingly lacking in low-speed torque'. You can only wonder what they would have made of the US version.

They liked the handling and the ride rather better, though, and remarked that:

On corners the car is very well balanced and what little understeer there is gets disguised by the power steering, making the car handle very neatly and responsively on twisting roads ... On ordinary roads the

Generously proportioned windscreen pillars were designed with the help of computers to provide roll-over protection and to deflect dirt from the side windows.

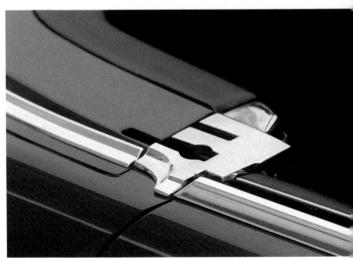

With the 350SL, Mercedes said farewell at last to rear-swing axles, and adopted this new semi-trailing arm layout, with the main elements carried on a strong subframe.

Attractive alloy wheels were an option for European customers.

Quality was still the main hallmark – as here in the superb finish around the doors and soft-top cover.

A totally redesigned dash for the 350SL was less stylized and more conventional. Manual transmission on a left-hand drive car was to become a rare choice.

The 300SL (this is a 1987 model) upgraded the six-cylinder SL line from 1985, using the excellent 3-litre engine first seen in the 300E saloon . . .

. . . as ever, it offered the versatility of hard- or soft-tops . . .

. . . and as ever, it had the unmistakable SL face.

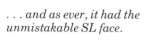

suspension feels surprisingly taut and firm, giving a rather lively ride . . . the suspension seems to soften up at speed, giving a level, well-damped and very comfortable ride . . .

As had their American colleagues, they did not want to call it a sports car, but concluded that they were impressed by other aspects of the new character: 'The 350SL proved less exciting than was expected. Instead, the emphasis was on comfort, safety and functional efficiency.'

FEW REASONS TO CHANGE

Without a doubt, Mercedes would not have been offended by the suggestion that the new SL was not a sports car, not given the tone of the rest of the reception. Nor were they in any great hurry to change anything they did not actually have to.

Of course, there would be a few things that did not leave them with much option. Even as launched, the 350SL 4.5 had been forced to use a rather unattractive twin, round headlight layout for the US market; next, for 1974, it had to comply with even tougher front and rear impact requirements, and that meant it had to adopt ugly bumpers which stuck out some 5in (12.5cm) at either end of the car. Mercedes, like many other manufacturers, knew these bumpers were ugly, but argued that they could not justify totally redesigning them for one market – and it has to be said that bad as the production bumpers looked, they did not look nearly so absurd as the monstrosities on Mercedes' ESF-05 'Experimental Safety Vehicle'. Mercifully, the fuel crisis of 1973 at least stopped the rash of heavy and clumsy 'safety vehicles' that seemed to be coming from all directions just prior to the squeeze.

In 1973 Mercedes did make one important rationalization in the SL range when they put the 4½-litre engine into the European car. After that model had been unveiled at the Geneva show in March (and reached Britain in May), both the US and European versions became known simply as the 450SL. With a bit less restriction in the breathing and ignition, the European 4½-litre engine produced 225bhp (DIN), but an illustration of how violently the oil crisis (and the removal of the fixed-dollar exchange rate in 1971) had changed world money markets, the UK price, in barely two years, had gone from less than £5,500 for the 350SL to almost £8,500 for the 450SL, and it was still rising dramatically.

THE FRUGAL ALTERNATIVES

Prices apart, the 1973 capacity increase was the last fundamental change to hit the SL for several years, but there was something else. Not so much a change as an addition, in 1974 Mercedes did spring the surprise of a new six-cylinder 280SL, exclusively for the European market.

It was an impressively rapid reaction to the 'energy crisis' of 1973, which had suddenly made a car which averaged only around 16mpg (5.7km per litre) seem something of a liability even to Mercedes customers, and a car which did 130mph (209kph) seem sadly unnecessary against a growing catalogue of supposedly fuel-saving speed limits.

Actually, this new variation on the 280 theme was by no means a second-rate alternative. Its 2.8-litre in-line six-cylinder engine was not the old 280SL one, but the elegant M110 type as introduced in the smaller S-class models early in 1972. It was a twin-cam unit with a seven-main-bearing crankshaft, which had full counterweighting plus a 'twin-mass' torsional damper to give exceptional smoothness even for the inherently smooth in-line six-cylinder layout. It had a cross-flow cylinder head with the exhausts on the left and the inlets on the right, the latter fed by a high-pressure injection system, and it used electronic ignition with a built in rev-limiter.

It was a lighter engine than the iron-blocked 3½-litre V8 of the 350SL, yet it gave away very little in terms of power. From 2,746cc it produced 185bhp (DIN) at 5,800rpm, compared to the 200bhp of big brother. To many ears, it even sounded crisper and if anything *more* sporty. What is more, as used in the 280SL, it could be had with a five-speed manual gearbox, which was something the V8s did not offer.

With a somewhat lower final drive ratio than the V8-engined, auto-boxed models, a manual 280SL suffered surprisingly little performance penalty over a V8. According to Mercedes, it was only 3mph (5kph) slower than they had originally claimed for the 350SL, at 127mph (204kph), and less than a second slower to 60mph (97kph), which was claimed to take 9.5 seconds. It must be a reflection on what the SL and the SL buyer had become, though, that precious few cars were ever supplied with the do-it-yourself gearbox.

The 280SL was presented, of course, as being responsibly frugal rather than austere, because however much you feared you were about to pay for your petrol and however much you wanted to contribute to conserving it, it would not do to be seen skimping on the little luxuries. Slightly narrower tyres (in 185 series rather than 205) would contribute a tiny bit more to better consumption too, and would be quite big enough for the lighter car, but aside from that and the badge on the boot lid, there was nothing to suggest any move down market. The 280SLs were only a few hundred pounds cheaper than the V8s (the savings were supposed to be in fuel, not in purchase price) and in terms of trim and equipment they were virtually unchanged.

Interestingly, although the worst fears of the first oil crisis proved quite short-lived and did not threaten again until the 1980s,

the six-cylinder cars found their own niche and survived right through to the end of this SL generation in 1989. There was just one major updating, late in 1985, when the 280SL was supplanted by a new 300SL.

It had the new engine first seen in the 300E saloon in December 1984, which was widely regarded as one of the finest cars that Mercedes had built in many years. In effect, it was a six-cylinder version of the four-cylinder engine in the newly introduced 190 compact saloon range, and was considered by some to be the best in-line six-cylinder engine in the world. It had just a single overhead camshaft (still chain-driven where most competitors had long preferred belts), for compactness and light weight – but the valves were now in a wide vee and operated by rockers. With bore and stroke dimensions of 88.5 × 80.3mm, it displaced 2,962cc. Again with Bosch injection, it offered 180bhp (DIN) at 5,700rpm and the utmost smoothness and refinement. If there was a catch, it was that further updating of the SL shell had left it heavier still, and even more conspicuously so alongside the new generation of saloons, taking full advantage of developing design technology. The 350SL was now some 375lb (170kg) heavier than a 300E saloon . . .

LIGHTWEIGHT EIGHTS

Back with the V8s, as the world had eventually found out, the early 1970s 'energy crisis' was not the beginning of the end for the private automobile that many doom-mongers gleefully predicted, but it did have a positive long-term effect in making us all think a bit harder about efficiency and conservation.

Mercedes actually turned that into a positive marketing stance with their 'Energy Concept' cars of the early 1980s, and by the mid-1970s they were already moving in that direction. In September 1977 they had added a completely new engine to the range in

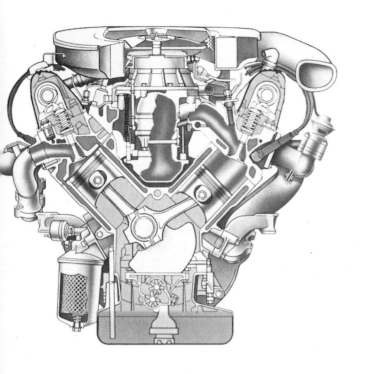

The biggest change in the lifetime of the V8 generation came with the change from iron to aluminium V8s, as part of Mercedes' 'Energy Concept' programme. There were those, however, who pointed out that the amount of energy needed to build the aluminium engines far outweighed even long-term fuel savings.

(Opposite) The bonnet, boot lids and even the bumpers were in aluminium to make a token inroad into the substantial weight.

The 5-litre alloy-engined 500SL in European specification was the ultimate 1980s generation SL, easily recognizable by the neat lip spoiler on the boot lid.

another step towards bringing the cars into line with modern requirements. It was part of the programme for making the bigger saloons lighter and more fuel efficient, but it would not appear in those until 1979; in fact Mercedes put it first of all into the low-volume SLC coupé, which thereby gained the label 450SLC 5.0, and having proved that it worked, they put it into the 500SL in 1980.

As the badge suggested, capacity had gone up to 5 litres, but the main difference with this engine was that it was now largely aluminium rather than cast iron, and thus a great deal lighter. Externally, its dimensions were much the same as the 450 V8, but in spite of the necessarily more comprehensive internal stiffening, it weighed almost 90lb (41kg) less than the older cast-iron engine.

The new block, heads and even cam covers were all cast in aluminium alloy. The block was cast in a high-silicon alloy and the bores were then chemically etched to reveal the silicon structure, which thus provided a low-friction surface in which the plated pistons and rings could run without the need for an intermediate liner. That made the construction lighter, eliminated problems of thermal expansion and left room to increase the bore size to achieve additional capacity – bore and stroke being 96.5 × 85.0mm and capacity 4,973cc. Slightly bigger valves were added and the new engine, naturally with Bosch injection, gave 240bhp at 5,000rpm and 298lb ft of torque at 3,200rpm.

Visually, the 500s were distinguished mainly by a deeper front spoiler (which was extremely neat and did have a worthwhile aerodynamic effect in tidying up the front under-body airflow) and a vestigial lip-type spoiler along the rear edge of the boot lid. The latter, like the bonnet and bumpers, had now reverted to aluminium in an attempt to lose a bit more weight.

Launched in Britain in October 1980, with a price-tag of some £20,300, the 500SL

was accepted as a big step forward, and *Motor* concluded:

There are few who will argue – we included – that the 500SL is one of the world's finest luxury sports cars; beautifully styled and superbly engineered. Its engine and automatic transmission set extremely high standards in terms of smoothness and refinement while in most conditions its handling and roadholding are of the highest order . . .

In an odd reversal of previous form, America did not get the 500SL, nor even (yet) a bigger version as palliative to its myriad restrictions; eventually it got the new all-alloy V8 but in a *smaller* guise. And Europe even got that before America did, at the same time as the 500 in 1980. As the new 5-litre alloy V8 had replaced the 450SL, this smaller, 3.8-litre version was evolved into the 380SL and took the place of the 350SL, which had been running happily alongside the bigger car in Europe since early 1973.

MORE FROM LESS

For Europe, the 3,839cc V8 had initially had the big bore/short stroke configuration that helped liberate high revs and high power, in this case 218bhp at 5,500rpm. However, by the time it arrived in America in 1982 (in the 380SL which would take the place of the 450SL), it had been juggled around to keep the same capacity but with smaller bores and longer stroke, plus numerous revisions to cylinder heads and manifolds, and revised electronic management. All that, of course, was in deference to improving economy and emissions control, and came at the expense of reducing maximum power to 155bhp at a miserably uninspiring 4,750rpm. As ever, the only way the US specification engine stood up reasonably well was in its slogging torque, which for the 380SL was quoted as 196lb ft at only 2,750rpm.

Unfortunately, you might say, in line with Mercedes' 1982 'Energy Concept', that longer stroke layout then filtered back to Europe too, so everyone had an engine of 88.0 × 78.9mm, and even if the European version did not slip back to US power levels and did gain better economy, it lost a lot of its free-revving character.

America did not seem to mind the erosion of the sporting side; the SL was now very simply a high-prestige toy for the very rich. By the start of the 1980s, the US price of a 450SL had rocketed to over $36,100, but in 1980 Mercedes-Benz of North America would sell no less than 6,129 roadsters – a figure which had varied remarkably little however prices and image had changed. True, it had gained odd refinements like automatic climate control and cruise control, but now it was inescapably over three times the launch price for rather less performance.

What is more, the 155bhp 380SL was not such a backward step as it might sound, not when you stop to consider what the outgoing 450SL had become in its latter years. Further sops to tightening emissions laws (especially in California where the climate guaranteed a strong market for open-topped cars) had reduced power output first to 180bhp and latterly to a miserably strangled 160bhp at a lethargic 4,200rpm. The latest damage was done by new and even milder camshafts, revised pistons and different exhaust manifolds. Although the change from a two-way to a three-way catalyst with oxygen sensor allowed some of the earlier, cruder emissions equipment to be dispensed with, there was no attempt to hold power up. That was no longer seen as relevant in a country which had a 55mph (90kph) blanket speed limit.

At the same time, the overall gearing (still with three-speed automatic as standard) had been made much taller, not to improve maximum speed, of course, but to improve cruising fuel consumption. It did that by as much as 30 per cent, but the 0–60mph (0–97kph) time had been slapped back to almost 12 seconds and the top speed was hardly over 110mph (177kph).

The 450SL was also now being described more and more often as out of date, or even in one case 'vintage', but in almost the same breath it was also called 'one of the world's great automotive status symbols'. At the same time there were regular mentions of an all-new successor on the way, delayed only by more pressing projects.

DIFFERENT STROKES

As the 380SL did not arrive in America until some two years after it was first shown off at the Geneva show in March 1980, it was not quite as 'all-new' as they might have been expecting, but it was at least rather better than the 450 had become. Yes, it only had 155bhp compared to the original European figure of 218bhp, but it did have that 196lb ft of torque and immense flexibility, and the engine alone was some 110lb (50kg) lighter than the old US 4.5-litre.

The rest of the car was also a touch lighter thanks to more aluminium panels, and it now offered the latest (start-in-first) four-speed automatic transmission with torque converter and an even taller final-drive ratio.

The net result was that it was just a blink quicker to 60mph (97kph) than the last, 160bhp 450SL, progressively slower at higher speeds and only a couple of mph behind on maximum speed – but with a small improvement in fuel economy and a big one in emissions. Departments like handling and ride were now described as good rather than outstanding, but, amazingly perhaps, *Road & Track*'s summing up in 1982 had a familiar ring: 'If it's a well built, luxurious two-seat open car with hard and soft tops, a big V8 engine, automatic transmission and power assists you're looking for, look no farther – this is your one and

The 420SL replaced the 380 in 1985, with many improvements beyond the increase in engine size. Styling features like the side ribs (which also helped keep the doors clean) were naturally continued.

'Just the thing for the lady or gentleman wanting luxury, reliability, status . . .'

One of the more obvious changes was to bigger wheels with lower profile tyres, improving handling and looks.

Behind the deep-spoilered nose, the 420SL had gained further suspension revisions and bigger, more powerful brakes, now with ABS as standard.

A read-out of 160mph (260kph) on the speedo may have been a bit optimistic for the 420SL, but the range was still holding its sporty image.

The latest automatic transmissions as in this 1987 420SL had dual-mode control.

The easiest way of distinguishing one SL from another was still in the understated badging.

only choice.' The latest east coast price tag, incidentally, was just over $39,300, and if America looked longingly at the European 500SL, that was as much as they could do officially, because the bigger engined car was not for sale in the USA. That, of course, was not to say that the grey market could not find you one, and in later years the number of 'unofficial' imports of 500SLs probably rather embarrassed Mercedes.

THE BIGGEST SLs

For Europe, a 4.2-litre 420SL replaced the 3.8-litre 380 in 1985, alongside the continuing but further improved 5-litre 500SL; and, as already described, the 2.8-litre six-cylinder 280SL grew into the excellent 3-litre single-cam six-cylinder 300SL. In each case those were the largest of the European SL families. The 4,196cc 4.2 engine was essentially a 3.8 with bigger bores, but it had several improvements in the cylinder heads too, with bigger valves and better porting, complemented by the latest generation of engine management, which gave it 218 bhp at 5,200rpm and 243lb ft of torque. The latter changes reflected improvements in the 5-litre engine, which, with revised camshafts, improved its output to no less than 245bhp and thus became the most powerful SL so far.

As well as being given the new engines, the whole range was updated for 1986 and more so, perhaps, than meets the eye. The improvements started with bigger diameter wheels carrying wider but lower profile tyres at 205/65VR15. As well as offering a significant improvement in grip, they also at last took away the car's slightly under-tyred look. More importantly, the new wheels made space for slightly bigger front brake discs, with four-pot callipers. At the front, the SL was given the suspension geometry of the latest S-class saloons. ABS braking became standard on all SL models, and the

latest automatic transmissions featured two control modes, allowing a choice between Sport and Economy, which essentially just varied the full-throttle change-up points.

And America finally got the bigger SL that it had sometimes craved and, as it turned out, it was the biggest of all of them. Launched in 1986, by which time the coming of another generation was already an open secret, it was just the sort of car that America loved.

THE $48,000 HOT ROD

Introducing it, *Road & Track* commented:

In fact, just when we'd begun to think the SL was getting a little long in the tooth (our thoughts encouraged, no doubt, by spy photos of its replacement), what does Mercedes do but turn it into something of a hot rod. Here's a car that used to be sedate now being capable, for example, of beating a Ferrari Mondial Cabriolet in a drag race.

What gave the SL this new (if only short-lived) lease on life? Something known to hot-rodders since the first one peered thoughtfully into the engine compartment of his Ford roadster: a simple infusion of cubic inches. Only here, dollars and Deutsche Marks help too.

The dollars side had now gone up to a staggering $48,600, and the simple infusion of cubic inches that it brought with it was the exchange of the 3.8-litre V8 for one of virtually 5.6 litres, to create the 560SL for US consumption only.

This fuel-injected, 96.5 × 94.8mm, 5,547cc engine put the 155bhp 380SL comprehensively in the shade, with 227 bhp at 4,750rpm and 279lb ft of torque at 3,250rpm, to give America a taste of the sort of power European SL owners had long enjoyed. It was coupled with the four-speed and torque-converter auto, the latest front suspension geometry, the latest torque-compensating rear axle layout with reduced squat and lift, a limited-slip differential and ABS brakes – though, surprisingly perhaps, nothing more than the normal current 205/65VR15 tyre wear – Mercedes once again proving themselves to be staunchly conservative in resisting ultra-wide rubber.

Leather upholstery was standard too, with a bit more padding to encourage further moans about the cabin now feeling cramped, but still no electric seat adjustment, even though there were such exotic items as thermostatically heated windscreen washer nozzles, a built-in anti-theft system, and a totally superfluous 'economy gauge'. There was also now an air bag to supplement the seat belts, showing how far safety consciousness had come in the fifteen years since the 350SL's inertia-reel belts seemed novel. It had the new deeper front dam, and the old and still fearfully ugly 5mph (8kph) bumpers and quad headlights.

The car was, not too surprisingly, the quickest SL that America had had of late – if still, ironically, some way behind the original SL for maximum speed. It would do around 130mph (209kph) and 0–60mph (0–97kph) in 7½ seconds, and that was accepted as good in the mid-1980s US scheme of things. *Road & Track*, in a road test sub-titled 'There's no substitute for cubic dollars', concluded:

The SL is an intriguing blend of the state of the art and the outdated. And, whatever your view of this blend, it sells quite well: some 7,600 in the first nine months of 1985; 6,030 in a German-strike-limited 1984. Considered a response to the grey market, our 560SL is unique to the North American continent; Europeans make do with the 500SL, whose 5.0-litre powerplant is just about equivalent to the 560's in US trim.

The SL has carved an enviable niche for itself as a town and touring car for the well-to-do; conservative, yet a trifle ostentatious; understated, but a little pretentious. 'Just

the thing,' noted one of the staff, 'for the lady or gentleman wanting luxury, reliability, status – and lots of V8 power'.

'It's a middle-aged hot rod,' summed up another, 'and it sure surprises a lot of folks not used to seeing Mercedes driven with some verve.'

A GRACIOUS ENDING

After eighteen years, though, the third generation SLs were finally into their last phase, yet they were still selling well. By the time the final models were being sold, British prices had risen to some £32,750 for a six-cylinder 300SL and to no less than £41,700 for a 500SL – the latter not far short of eight times the £5,457 cost of the first 350SL. For all that, demand for the SLs had never slackened. From 1971 to 1989, total production of all models (including the longer wheelbase, fixed head SLCs) amounted to 237,287 cars, and of those, 14,522 came to Britain. Numerically, that made it far and away the most successful of all the SLs, and that was perhaps all the more surprising given the unsettled period through which it was on sale with oil crises, safety lobbying and economic downturns.

While all this was going on, everyone with an interest in the breed was aware that the next generation of SLs was already well under way, and great things were clearly expected – more, as it turned out, and rather sooner than Mercedes were eventually to deliver, as expected introduction dates began to slip very close to the end of the decade.

The last of the third generation SLs was built in Stuttgart on 4 August 1989 at the Bremen plant after production of the new model had already started. It was destined to go into the Daimler-Benz museum, while the world in general prepared its rave reviews for the next car.

The SLCs

Alongside the soft-top SLs of the third generation, Mercedes built a closely-related family of four-seater, fixed hard-top coupés, the SLCs. They were something of a surprise replacement for the bigger, older, saloon-based coupé line, but they ran for nine years from 1972 to 1981, before they were in turn replaced by a 'dedicated' coupé range, which was once again based on shortened saloons rather than on lengthened sports cars.

Although they were perhaps sometimes misunderstood as being a compromise of the SL philosophy, the SLCs were in reality exceptionally fine cars in their own right.

The coupés were built in 280SLC, 350SLC (350SLC 4.5 in the USA, of course), 450SLC and 450SLC 5.0 versions, and they were in most ways directly based on the equivalent SLs. The original models had been designed in parallel with each other, rather than the SLCs just being a conversion job.

They had the same engines, transmissions and suspensions, and, viewed directly from the front or back, almost identical looks. The big differences were only apparent from the side, in that the wheelbase was increased by 14in (36cm) (from 97in, or 246cm, to 111in, or 282cm) to accommodate proper rear seats, and the hard-top was a permanent one, with a marginally taller roof line to turn the SLCs into true coupés. They still only had two doors, but the rear seats were genuinely big enough to take two (and at a pinch three) adults in considerable comfort over more or less any distance – luggage space was slightly improved accordingly.

The extra length was between the rear of the doors and the front of the rear wheelarches, and in the roof line the potentially awkward look of a much longer rear window was avoided by adding some distinctive louvres ahead of the rear pillars and behind the wind-up quarter windows. From the outside they appeared solid, but from the inside they were cleverly angled to be barely noticeable over the rear glass.

The SLCs were unavoidably somewhat heavier than the two-seaters, but not by much, so straight-line performance suffered very little; Mercedes claimed a top speed of around 140mph (225kph) and 0–60mph (0–97kph) in under 8½ seconds. As for drivability, in that the wheelbase was a little longer than the two-seater, they were maybe a bit less agile on very tight roads, but the ride comfort and balance were often remarked as being even better than those of the SL. What is more, the fixed roof could only have made the SLC stiffer than the open-topped SLs, and that made the handling at least as good, and to some observers actually better.

The choice of six-cylinder and V8 engines for the SLC directly mirrored that for the SL.

For the driver, little had changed.

On that basis, maybe it is less surprising that the SLCs had something of a competition career – not directly involving the factory, of course, but there was always plenty of advice and assistance for the several privateers who rallied (and occasionally raced) the coupés. Tony Fowkes did well in British rallying in the mid-1970s with a 450SLC, but the car's most spectacular success was in winning the tough 1978 South American Rally, driven by Andrew Cowan and Colin Malkin. It was one of four SLCs in the event, which passed through ten countries over more than 18,000 miles (28,967km). The cars had to be near standard except for safety and durability equipment and careful preparation, and the SLC literally won quite comfortably.

The factory did not admit that they were directly intended to help those who campaigned SLCs, but at the Frankfurt show in September 1977 they launched a lightweight 5-litre version, the 450SLC 5.0, with the new all-alloy V8, alloy wheels, and alloy boot and bonnet lids. It saved more than 200lb (91kg) over the normal 450SLC, had 240bhp which made it quite a rapid device, and was almost ten per cent more slippery too, with the new deep front spoiler and the little lip on the boot lid.

The competition cars represented only a tiny fringe of SLC success, of course, and the production models did pretty well in overall sales terms. Mercedes sold a total of over 45,000 350 and 450 cars in that relatively short life-span for example, although the underpowered 280 and rather specialized 5-litre admittedly did not contribute many more to that total. In the end, the SLCs disappeared mainly because the reappearance of saloon-based coupés simply offered a better way of reaching the same market.

8 An SL for the 1990s

The opening lines of *Autocar & Motor*'s first full road test on the newly-available-in-Britain 500SL in December 1989 read:

Compare the new SL with the 18-year-old model it replaces and you could believe that hidden away in some secret part of Mercedes' Stuttgart factory there sits a still-born SL: the missing link.

Such is the advance made by the company with the new car. It furthers Mercedes' ground-breaking safety record and at the same time shows that the company's stifling conservatism is at last giving away to flair and imagination. The SL is the most dramatic – some would say indulgent – production Mercedes since the gullwing 300SL . . .

Not far short of two full years earlier, in February 1987, the magazine had had photographs of a virtually undisguised new SL on its cover, on test prior to what was expected to be its début at the Frankfurt show later in 1987. Only a relatively under-stated false nose and boot lid spoiler plus some spurious trim strips on the flanks looked noticeably different from the way the car eventually appeared, although the headlight and turn indicator units looked slightly cobbled together. The issue was headlined 'Exposed! Merc's new flagship. The coupé class of '88 . . . '

The story hinted that with the news that BMW's expected 6-Series coupé was being delayed, Mercedes were intent on seizing the initiative in this high-profile battle.

With that dramatic wedge profile and obviously flush glass all round, the magazine was not taking too many chances in predicting a drag factor down in the order of 0.34Cd. They were further adrift, however, with their engine predictions which started, correctly as it turned out, with a 3-litre six-cylinder, but continued with a new version of the 4.2-litre V8, a 32-valve development of the mighty 5.6-litre V8, and a 5.2-litre V12 engine. *Car* magazine had photographs of the car on winter test in Scandinavia and made virtually exactly the same predictions, V12 included.

The engine, in fairness, had been expected from Daimler-Benz for some time – although there were doubts that it would ever actually happen; the marketing men wanted it more than the engineers did (to challenge BMW and Jaguar), while the engineers thought they could already do that with their best V8s. Other predictions from *Autocar & Motor* included height-adjustable suspension, four-wheel drive and anti-skid systems, which like most of their subsequent detail suggestions were impressively close to the mark.

A LONG TIME COMING

All this is rather jumping the gun, however, because the one thing that proved to be considerably over-optimistic was that late-1987 launch date. By the time Mercedes finally did launch the car and the magazine finally did get to drive it in UK trim late in 1989, that comment about missing links in the depths of Stuttgart was particularly apposite. There had certainly been time for any number of interim models during the fourth generation SL's gestation.

In their own introduction to the car, the design team who had worked on it for so

300SL-24, 1989–

Body type	:	two-door, two-seater roadster with powered folding soft-top and removable hard-top
Chassis	:	platform with unitary body
Engine type	:	in-line six-cylinder
Capacity	:	2,962cc
Bore	:	88.5mm
Stroke	:	80.2mm
Compression ratio	:	10.0:1
Cylinders	:	alloy block, seven main bearings
Cylinder head	:	alloy, four valves per cylinder operated by twin, chain-driven, overhead camshafts, with variable inlet camshaft timing
Fuel system	:	Bosch KE5 CIS electronic injection
Maximum power	:	231bhp at 6,300rpm
Maximum torque	:	201lb ft at 4,600rpm
Bhp per litre	:	78.0
Gearbox type	:	four-speed automatic with torque converter and selectable modes (five-speed automatic and five-speed manual optional)
Gear ratios	:	(Fifth: 0.75) Second: 2.25 Fourth: 1.00 First: 3.87 Third: 1.44 Reverse: 5.59
Final drive ratio	:	3.69:1
Clutch	:	n/a
Front suspension	:	strut type with lower wishbones, coil springs, telescopic gas-filled dampers, anti-roll bar
Rear suspension	:	multi-link, coil springs, telescopic gas-filled dampers, anti-roll bar, optional self-levelling control
Brakes	:	ventilated front discs with four-piston callipers, solid rear discs with two-piston callipers; servo assistance; ABS anti-lock system
Steering	:	recirculating ball, with power assistance
Wheels and tyres	:	alloy; 225/55ZR16 radial-ply tyres
Overall length	:	176.0in (447.0cm)
Overall width	:	71.3in (181.2cm)
Overall height	:	50.5in (129.3cm)
Wheelbase	:	99.0in (251.5cm)
Track	:	60.3in (153.2cm)
Ground clearance	:	6.0in (15.2cm)
Fuel tank capacity	:	21.1gal (80 litres)
Unladen weight	:	3,718lb (1,690kg)
Power to weight ratio	:	139.2bhp/ton

PERFORMANCE

Maximum speed	:	143mph (230kph)
0–60mph (0–97kph)	:	8.1sec
0–100mph (0–161kph)	:	22.0sec
Standing ¼ mile (0.4km)	:	16.4sec
Fuel consumption	:	approx 20mpg (7.1km per litre)

*'The SL is the most dramatic – some would say indulgent – production
Mercedes since the Gullwing 300SL . . .'*

long before it took its first public bow
acknowledged that by admitting, 'This is the
most difficult and challenging task we have
ever faced.'

From Mercedes, such frankness does not
come flippantly. The new family when it did
appear comprised three models: the baseline
300SL with 190bhp single-overhead camshaft straight six; the 300SL-24, also with a
3-litre straight-six but in this case a new
engine with twin overhead camshafts, four
valves per cylinder and 231bhp; and the
flagship 5-litre, 326bhp V8-engined 500SL.
There was no sign of the 4.2 V8, the 32-valve
5.6 or the V12, but two out of those three
were no longer expected, and it was known
that the V12 would not arrive until later,
and then in the S-class saloons.

All three versions of the new SL shared a
stunningly clean and classic look; a look
that was modern and distinctive yet every
inch the embodiment of Mercedes style.
Between them they were bristling with
more technological innovations than any
Mercedes before them. In other words, they
were typical SLs almost in the manner of the
first generation.

The delay to the car's launch was less to do
with technical problems than with sheer
pressure of work at Stuttgart as the company started into their second century; final
detail work on type R129 had to be fitted in
around consolidation of the smaller, W201
saloon range (the 190s), the launch of the
mid-sized W124s (the new 200/300 series)
and development of the new S-class (including

the V12-engined flagship). By the time the three SLs were launched, at the Geneva Motor Show in March 1989, the new family had been more than ten years in the making, and once again virtually everything was new except the badge.

When the programme to create the new model was started, it was decided that it should combine the most advanced styling with 'a gentle reminder of the SL tradition'. By the time the car was launched, that would be a tradition stretching back some thirty-five years; even when the planning started, the SL family was already around a quarter of a century old, yet it had really only gone through those three production generations. Mercedes do not work to quite the same model replacement schedules as some lesser companies.

And so the latest SL design team, led by chief stylist Bruno Sacco, started from the basis that the new car not only had to bear a family affinity with the 1971–89 generation of SLs that it would directly supersede, but also had to keep faith with the philosophy of the original Gullwing – as a sports car with sophistication. In that it was being formulated during the mid- to late 1970s and

Magnificently aggressive front-end styling of the latest SLs shows how Mercedes attacked the car with no thoughts of toning down the muscle-car image.

through the 1980s, it had to fit a number of other new criteria too, connected with both social conscience and ever-tougher world-wide legislation – both stemming from the oil crises of the 1970s and early 1980s.

On previous form, and again in keeping with Mercedes tradition, they also had to consider it as a design with a long produc-tion life ahead of it, during which the last thing that should happen was that it should ever start to look dated or gauche. Accord-ingly, they aimed for what they described as 'a timeless appeal – modern and fresh but without fads which could quickly render the concept out of date in a world of rapidly changing aesthetics'.

They would go for a distinctive shape, with the classic SL proportions of long nose, short tail and compact roof section, and let details like the radiator grille and air vents behind the front wheels evoke the earlier models. As with all the earlier SLs, they would be creating a series of body styles – hard-top and soft-top – each of which had to work equally well and date with the same good grace. Performance still had to be part of the recipe, but performance with the maximum possible attention to active and passive safety. And, even more than ever before, so did luxury and limousine-like comfort – SL drivers today are not frustrated racers any more, they are sophisticated peo-ple who have made their mark, who can afford the best and who expect nothing less from a Mercedes, even if it is a sporty one.

1970s BEGINNINGS

First thoughts for Type R129, the SL to take Mercedes not only into the 1990s but hope-fully into the twenty-first century too, were taking shape even before the 1970s had ended – if not with detailed design work, then at least in studying the competition and trying to rationalize trends for the future.

And tradition did not mean rejecting

progress; that had never been the Stuttgart way. In the earliest days, in fact, Mercedes even considered building a mid-engined SL for the 1990s. That may sound uncharacteristically extreme, but had it materialized, it would probably have seemed no more revolutionary to 1990s eyes than the original 300SL Gullwing coupé had to 1950s ones.

Nor was it without some precedent; Mer-cedes had built several versions of the experimental mid-engined C111 coupés between 1969 and 1979, with Wankel engines, turbo-diesels and finally twin-turbo petrol V8s to take numerous high-speed, long-distance records, and a version of that car was a serious production temptation for quite some time. What is more, with Merce-des back into world class sports car racing with a vengeance in the late 1980s and early 1990s, they would have both extended the technology and created a viable marketing link with their new Le Mans winner.

The supercar fringe, however, was no lon-ger the expected niche for the most sporting Mercedes, so the mid-engined concept was put on hold at an early stage and the main thrust of design was switched to blending science with style.

By 1982, the ground rules were pretty effectively set and the style was evolving. Three approaches had originally been con-sidered and finally reduced to one. A strictly conventional approach (effectively not much more than a direct replacement for the third generation SLs) was rejected, as was the idea of a very futuristic model which would almost certainly have meant the mid-engined route. The concept that won the day was that of a thoroughly modern car but which had a touch of tradition.

TOWARDS A NEW STYLE

Early drawings from around 1981 show a radically different car, deeply slab-sided and

Part of the styling brief that has applied to almost all SLs is that the car should look equally good in three formats – hard-topped, soft-topped and open-topped.

very tall and square in the tail, which had a number of different treatments. In several of the more adventurous ones the rear wheelarches were partly or totally enclosed; in some of the renderings, the rear deck was flat, in some it formed a large spoiler, and in at least one it had a sliding, ribbed cover. Probably the most outrageous of all by Mercedes standards had two streamlined headrests behind the driver and passenger, in a style that was a cross between the old 300SLRs and any number of motor show concept cars, from the early 1950s to the present day. One of the hard-top renderings looks very like a chunky two-door version of Citroën's big XM saloon, but any one of them would probably have dated a good deal more quickly than the later, more conservative designs.

By 1983, the drawings showed a softer, rounder approach, but the proportions still had not quite gelled, especially in the roof

line. The marked rearward slope of the nose, though, was evident in most of the drawings, and even went back as far as some studies for a Wankel rotary-engined successor for the earlier cars, dating from around the middle of 1968.

It is not difficult, either, to see those cosmetic tricks for evoking the old cars – from the inevitable side vents to neat versions of the small aerodynamic strakes above the wheelarch openings.

From the drawings, Sacco and his team progressed to the model stage, and almost twenty one-fifth scale renderings were built, followed in several cases by full-sized versions in clay, wood or plastic. The roof line in particular was proving difficult to finalize while complying with the safety aspects of the original design brief, and no less than thirty-four styles were tried, including one finned version with a rigid roll-bar. Finally, it was decided that the car would have a retractable, flip-up roll-bar, which added mechanical complexity but meant the styling of the roof line did not have to be compromised.

By 1985, the whole of the basic design of the new SL was finalized, and between then and the launch, it changed only in detail and refinement rather than in any fundamental aspect. Mercedes, as mentioned, were already heavily committed in the interim with all those other pressing projects from entry-level saloon to V12 S-Class, the latter scheduled for a launch a couple of years after the SL.

SIMPLE AND EFFECTIVE

The beautiful shape of the new SL is as simple as could be, a subtle aerodynamic wedge that starts from that slanting, elegantly rounded nose line, and ends in the high, short tail. The steep rake and ultra-smooth construction of the screen and A-pillars give it further emphasis. Mercedes aver that the basic shape of the grille harks back as far as the 1930s, but it has never looked neater than in this version, with its anodized aluminium slats (finished in all cases in titanium anthracite) supporting a suitably large and immodest three-pointed star in the centre of the grille.

The detailing around the nose is exquisite, from the beautiful curves of headlight and indicator mouldings to the total integration of the bumper, fog lamps and lower skirts. The bumpers also have deformable exterior coverings, designed to absorb minor impacts and smooth enough not to be a threat to either pedestrians or aerodynamics.

The roof is low and the rear quarters very compact, giving the car the distinctive and desirable image of a beast about to pounce. The tail is every bit as smooth and tidy as the nose, tapering in quite dramatically in plan view, from the widest part of the body around the rear arches, and with the instantly recognizable Mercedes styling trademark of deeply ribbed 'stay-clean' light lenses

Almost all temptation to adornment was resisted. There are no add-on spoilers or separate trim-strips, just a thoroughly understated smoothness and elegance. Even the wheels are an understated design – marginally more conservative, in fact, than Bruno Sacco would really have liked, but occasionally even the design chief has to bow to the marketing men. The bumper line continues through the lower body flanks in a body-toned protector strip, not only to save the shell from stone chips and minor knocks but also to lighten the look of the otherwise plain slab sides.

The only touch of indulgence is the small vents behind the front wheelarches, reminiscent of the original SLs and also functional; and if you think them an unnecessary touch of stylistic licence, try visualizing this car without them . . .

EFFORT-FREE VERSATILITY

The latest SLs are once again two cars in one, offering both the detachable hard-top and the superbly well fitted soft-top for maximum versatility. In each case, attachment and operation of the tops is now completely automatic and demands little more from the driver than the touch of a button, although the weight of the fully-trimmed hard-top does still demand a helper to lift it fully on and off the car – at about 75lb (34kg) it is no lightweight, even though it is now made in aluminium rather than steel.

Lifting assistance apart, all that is necessary to release the top is to put the transmission selector in park and the parking brake on, detach the plug connector for the heated rear screen, switch on the ignition and pull back the red switch in the centre console. The roof unlocks within a couple of seconds

The short, aerodynamically clean tail
of the 300SL-24.

Super-neat detail finish and installation for
the excellent 24-valve 3-litre engine. A V8 is
a tight fit in the same space.

Sacco's team used details and proportions to
evoke the SL tradition, as in the long nose
with its dramatically sloping grille . . .

. . . and especially the neat and functional
side vents.

In three-rotor Wankel rotary engined guise, this 1969 version of the C111 coupé looks much closer to a production possibility than some of the C111 record breakers.

and all that remains is to lift it carefully from its mounts and find somewhere to store it – this remains a garage manoeuvre rather than an on-the-road one, as there is obviously no way to store the removed top on board the car.

Replacing the top is a simple reverse of the removal process, involving nothing more challenging than lining up the mountings and fixing points, and pushing the button in the other direction; the on-board locking systems even recognize the difference between hard-top and soft-top.

In the case of the soft-top, the process is even simpler, because you do not need a helper and you do not need a separate storage facility; Mercedes provide the equivalent of both, with the aid of fifteen hydraulic motors, forty-five hydraulic lines, seventeen microswitches and a central processor. Pull the switch in the same way as with the hard-top, and the hood unlocks itself at front and rear, lifts forward from the back edge to allow the steel lid of the storage compartment behind the cockpit to open, folds itself

neatly into the space and has the lid close back neatly over it – all within the space of barely thirty seconds. The hood itself is double layered and is as neat, draught- and flap-proof as you could wish, even around three-figure speeds.

With the soft-top stowed, the driver can protect himself and front-seat passenger from the ravages of wind on the back of the neck by raising the roll-bar and fitting the optional 'windjammer' (a remarkably effective fine-mesh screen) across it and letting the hugely powerful heating and ventilating system do the rest. The only catch with that is that if you are using the small rear seats for the traditional two children or one transversely mounted adult, you have to do without the windjamming net.

The interior of the latest SLs goes a giant step beyond even the patent luxury of the previous generation – in fact to levels that would disgrace virtually any limousine, except perhaps another Mercedes. The cabin trim is dominated by leather, polished wood and deep pile carpets, but aside from the luxury materials, modern technology abounds again.

The seats are typically Mercedes in shape, in that they are obviously designed to accommodate even the largest and best fed of German businessmen without appearing skimpy, but in themselves they have as much mechanical sophistication as do some entire cars. Mercedes described them as the most advanced seat ever produced for a production car.

They are built up from a fully load-bearing cast magnesium base, and with no less than five built-in motors they incorporate ten-way electrical adjustment for the reach, height, back-rest rake and head-rest height (all operated by Mercedes' brilliantly simple and logical 'model-seat' switchgear in each door panel). Three programmable memory positions are available at the touch of the appropriate button, and the driver's

seat memories are also complemented. by automatic adjustment of the steering wheel position and the positions of internal and external mirrors.

GEARED TO SAFETY

The seats have the option of two-stage heating and pneumatic lumbar adjustment too, and more fundamentally, as standard they incorporate the inertia reel seat belts – with no direct attachment to the bodyshell, only to the massively engineered seat frames themselves. That avoids the problem of being stuck with fixed-height (and rather low) upper belt anchorages on the top of the rear door posts, due to the fact that there is no proper B-pillar on the SL. Moreover, the completeness of the thinking is shown by the fact that the height of the upper belt

The mid-engined C111 was thoroughly developed over a fairly long period and there is little doubt that it must have been a serious temptation for Mercedes to put the gullwinged car into production.

mounting adjusts automatically with the head-rest. The seats also give warning if the backs are not properly secured when the doors are closed, for instance if someone has just moved them to climb into the back seats. A pneumatic device actually closes the seat to its final position for locking.

The other instantly noteworthy piece of safety-inspired high-tech is the retractable roll-bar. Normally, this substantial steel hoop, encased in polyurethane foam and beautifully trimmed, sits flush with the tonneau around the back of the rear seats and ahead of the hood stowage – unless the driver chooses to bring it up manually to its erect position by means of the appropriate switch. If the bar is down, though, and the car senses an accident is imminent, the hoop flips up under spring loading and locks in position within 0.3 seconds.

It does so under the control of a system of sensors on the transmission tunnel and the rear axle, which trigger an electromagnetic release switch. The sensors detect that the car is moving, that it has exceeded a specified roll angle (of around 26 degrees) and that one suspension unit is on full extension (which implies that its wheel is about to leave the ground); in other words, that the car is in all probability about to roll. It will also react to the onset of a non-rolling accident if the accelerometers detect a deceleration of more than 4g either laterally or longitudinally. As well as flipping up the roll bar, the system also simultaneously locks the seat belts and unlocks the doors, leaving them firmly closed but readily openable by occupants or an outside rescuer.

That, of course, is last-resort safety thinking, but the basic design of the car is also immensely strong and sophisticated. The platform is entirely new and designed with the latest finite-element technology for maximum rigidity with minimum weight. The shell is mainly in steel but has some 4.6 per cent of its components by weight in light alloys, which is twice what the previous SLs had.

The frame and floor use high-strength steel, large cross-sectional support members and particularly rigid connections between the A-pillars and the front chassis rails. The front chassis legs are attached to the passenger compartment at three points on each side of the car – on the side members, at the transmission tunnel and to the bulkhead. There are large, crushable sections at the front and rear of the cockpit, and a 'safety cell' in the centre, such as Mercedes pioneered and patented in the early 1950s. The fuel tank is positioned above the rear axle, where it should be protected from most impacts and special attention is paid to side intrusion protection. This is through the design of the doors themselves with intrusion-resistant inner construction, of the door pillars and locks, and by a cross member at the base of the windscreen to deflect part of any side impact to the opposite side of the car, thus sharing the loads.

The doors are also designed so as not to jam closed even in very severe frontal impacts, and the inner door release uses a cable rather than a rigid linkage so it is more likely to be workable even if the door itself is buckled.

Although when the SL was being designed, the legislative emphasis was on survivability of direct frontal impacts, Mercedes also paid great attention to front-offset collisions, which in real-life situations are very much more common, and which are now seen as a much more meaningful test. In the SL's case, front-end cross-bracing distributes impact loads through a high-strength steel cross member and into the engine and radiator supports. In a frontal accident with very little offset, diagonal supports connecting the chassis legs to the base of the front wings absorb the energy and distribute it through the full width of the car. The legs are conical and use metal of varying thicknesses with carefully designed stiffened ridges which channel the crush forces from the front to the rear of the chassis members.

In the end, the conventional approach won, with the usual Mercedes emphasis on simple and slow-to-date lines.

The inevitable wedge shape is even more exaggerated in the latest SLs by the steep rake and ultra-smooth construction of the windscreen pillars.

According to Mercedes, the basic shape of the grille harks back as far as some 1930s models, but the details of lights and bumpers are defined by aerodynamic excellence.

The new SL was designed with safety as the first objective not only for its occupants but for other road users too, including pedestrians and cyclists, in line with modern thinking that car manufacturers have a responsibility to protect those outside of a car as well as those inside in the event of an accident. Foremost in that thinking are the smoothness and slope of the nose to minimize hip and chest injuries, the deformable bumper coverings, deformable areas on the tops of the wings, the steeply sloping windscreen and smooth A-pillars, recessed rain gutters and door handles and even the protective covering of the wiper arms.

FUNDAMENTAL EXCELLENCE

Structural considerations were as important in dictating final design as style was, and Mercedes did not allow that to be compromised by any unnecessary constraints on the manufacturing side. If the ideal solution took a bit longer to build and cost a few more Deutschmarks, so be it, it was still the ideal solution and that was what the SL buyer would be paying for.

Mechanically, of course, the latest generation SLs are far from being superficial updates; in their blend of quality engineering and considered use of state-of-the-art technology, they offer conclusive proof that Mercedes engineering is still among the most imaginative and accomplished in the world. In nuts and bolts terms as well as in looks, they are new virtually from the ground up.

That starts with 225/55R16Z tyres on 8J × 16in alloy wheels which, of course, are much the biggest ever used on an SL but typically conservative when seen alongside some 'supercars' of broadly comparable performance. The suspension is essentially taken from the mid-sized W124 saloons and coupés, but with considerable 'fine tuning' to suit the SL. At the front, you will find the familiar Mercedes strut-type layout with lower wishbones, coil springs, and separate gas-filled dampers, plus anti-roll bar. It is conceived along lines that Herr Uhlenhaut would still very much appreciate, with generous travel (more than 7½in, or 19cm), relatively soft springing and very well controlled damping. The lower damper mounting is further outboard than on other models and actually within the wheel well, and the SL has more anti-dive built into its front geometry than any other model.

At the back, there is the complex and outstandingly effective Mercedes multi-link layout, with no less than five links per side. Again, it uses coil springs, gas dampers and an anti-roll bar – which in this case is markedly thinner than the one on the front and has its ends made in a composite material to minimize unsprung weight. As at the front, it has that long travel, with firm control. The rear geometry, with a slight forward tilt of the main suspension carrier, incorporates anti-squat and anti-lift, and a degree of passive rear-wheel steering. In a fore-and-aft direction the bushes are designed to resist toe-in changes for optimum straight-line stability, but when the springs are compressed in roll there is sufficient compliance in the bushes of the lower control arms to allow a tiny and controlled amount of rear wheel toe-in, to help promote mild (and predictable) understeer.

On top of all that, there is a standard self-levelling system and the option of 'adaptive damping', which automatically switches between soft and firm settings through two intermediate stages depending on load. The response is virtually instantaneous – to the extent that inputs sensed at the front wheels at 60mph (97kph) are passed on to adjust the rear dampers before the rear wheels pass the same point on the road. Additionally, at anything over around 75mph (121kph), the ride height is automatically lowered by around ½in (1cm) to improve stability and reduce drag.

The proportions of the SLs are dominated by the low roof line and short, cleanly tucked-in tail, finished off, of course, with the usual slatted 'stay-clean' lenses. Bumpers and lower body cladding are beautifully integrated.

PROTECTION FROM FOLLY

Steering is by a power-assisted Mercedes recirculating ball system, with only three turns between locks and the usual ridiculously large wheel. The dual-circuit, vacuum-assisted brakes use ventilated discs at the front, with fixed four-pot callipers, and solid rear discs with two-pot callipers. Naturally, ABS anti-lock braking is standard, and in this case the ABS sensors which detect the onset of wheel locking also double up to detect the onset of wheelspin under power and operate an anti-skid control. That instructs the engine management to back off the power, and if necessary also gently applies some braking to the appropriate wheel.

What it effectively does is eliminate the possibility of too hefty an application of torque to the rear wheels at the wrong moment which would kick the tail into over-steer; that will reassure the vast majority of drivers and perhaps frustrate the hooligan few (perish the thought) who prefer the lurid, but almost invariably slower, tail-out approach. Compounding the frustration, perhaps, is the fact that the SL's chassis is now so supremely competent that any skilled driver could revel in it without much fear of being bitten. But SLs are not actually meant to be that kind of car any more . . .

That is certainly not to say that they are not sporting – very far from it. They have taken SL performance into a whole new area and from point to point they may well qualify as some of the fastest yet most comfortable and refined cars in the world. That comes from blending the outstanding chassis with as much usable power as most people could ever want.

Understated smoothness and elegance, with as little adornment as possible.
Even the wheels are as simple as the marketing men could have wished.

POWER BY CHOICE

Two sixes and a very advanced V8 give a range of power options from 190bhp to 326bhp, with a choice of manual and automatic transmissions depending on model – although Mercedes accept the fact that the mix is dominated by as much as 95 per cent take-up of automatics.

Entry level, if it is fair to apply the term to any SL, is the plain 300SL with single-overhead-camshaft, two-valve-per-cylinder, in-line-six type M103 engine – much as fitted to other cars in Mercedes' mainstream range but with revised combustion chamber shapes. It has bore and stroke dimensions of 88.5 × 80.2mm for a capacity of 2,962cc. With the latest Bosch KE5 CIS injection, electronic ignition and a 9.2:1 compression ratio, it produces 190bhp at 5,700rpm and 192lb ft of torque at 4,500rpm.

It comes with the choice of four-speed automatic or five-speed manual gearboxes, with a markedly higher final drive ratio for the automatic car. That blunts acceleration but helps make high-speed cruising a bit less flustered, and Mercedes claim the best figures for the manual car. In so far as even this lightest of the three SLs weighs a hefty 3,630lb (1,647kg) (for a frankly modest power-to-weight ratio of only 117bhp per ton), a claimed maximum of 140mph (225kph) and 0–60mph (0–97kph) in less than 9.5 seconds are pretty impressive, if not exactly earth shattering.

The middle range M104 six-cylinder has exactly the same bore and stroke dimensions for the same capacity, but it offers a lot more power and a much sportier character altogether than the two-valve six. This impressive newcomer is based on the same block as the baseline M103, but with a cross-flow, four-valve cylinder head, and twin chain-driven overhead camshafts. Large individual ports blend into pairs at the manifold end to allow the injector nozzles to be placed nearer the inlet valves, and there is the added refinement of variable inlet timing.

That offers the best of both worlds; four valves per cylinder are a well-proven way of producing top-end power but traditionally at the expense of low-speed lethargy. One way around that is to have different valve timing for high-speed and low-speed running, and that is what Mercedes have given to this engine.

It is a clever system, combining mechanical and electronic control to optimize top-end power and low-speed flexibility. The adjusting mechanism is fitted into the inlet camshaft's drive gear, driven conventionally enough by a duplex roller chain from the crankshaft. In this case, the camshaft gear is allowed a small degree of rotation relative to the camshaft itself. The position in which the gear meshes with the shaft is varied by a hydraulic piston, controlled by a magnetic valve which responds to information from the engine management unit in response to engine speed and load.

At idle, there is virtually no valve overlap, but as engine speed increases the inlet cam phase is adjusted automatically to give a progressively larger amount of overlap at high speeds. The result is better low-speed torque, smoother running, reduced emissions and lower fuel consumption, followed

by better mid-range torque and finally by improved peak power.

This engine produces over 20 per cent more power than the basic six-cylinder one, yet it weighs only about 45lb (20kg) more. It gives 231bhp at 6,300rpm and 201lb ft of torque at 4,500rpm, and with a gloriously sporty noise and feel – some would say sportier even than the bigger and more powerful top-of-the-range V8. Again, the 300SL-24, as this model is dubbed, offers the five-speed manual or four-speed automatic transmissions, but additionally there is the choice of a sophisticated new five-speed automatic with torque converter. Available on the 300SL-24 only, it is based on the four-speed unit used in the 300E, but with a planetary gear-set with brake and clutch added at the rear to offer an overdrive fifth ratio. Selection of fifth is controlled electronically and is blocked out until the car is doing over 50mph (80kph). The control response is altered too; a sensor measures the speed with which the driver lifts off the throttle, and if the driver lifts suddenly, the sensor avoids a too-sudden change-down.

With the extra-tall top gear, overall gearing can be reduced, to make the intermediate ratios usefully more sporty. The kick-down control is also a mixture of electronic and hydraulic, and allows a direct kick-down from fifth to second if so desired. The whole package combines to give better acceleration and quieter, more fuel-efficient high-speed cruising. This mid-range SL is a pretty impressive performer too, with a claimed maximum of 143mph (230kph) and 0–60mph (0–97kph) acceleration in only just over 8 seconds.

THE MIGHTIEST SL

For the time being the quickest SL of all is, of course, the 32-valve V8-powered 500SL, with four-speed automatic and no other choice. This superb M119 engine was new for the model, although it is based on the all-aluminium M117 unit as used in the S-class saloon and also in the older 500SL. For the new sporting flagship, it was given a spectacular boost in specification, with four cams and four valves per cylinder, the clever and effective variable inlet timing as described for the 24-valve six-cylinder engine, and usefully more power and torque. Bore and stroke are 96.5×85.0mm for a capacity of 4,973cc, and with Bosch injection and a 10.0:1 compression ratio it produces 326bhp at 5,500rpm and 332lb ft of torque at 4,000rpm.

The car that it sits in is the heaviest of the three SLs, at 3,894lb (1,766kg), but with this amount of power, the power-to-weight ratio is up to 188bhp per ton, and with what are obviously superbly chosen automatic gear ratios and change points, it is even quicker than that might suggest. The yardstick 0–60mph (0–97kph) time is now claimed to be almost exactly 6 seconds and maximum speed is artificially limited to 155mph (249kph) by the electronic management; Mercedes, like BMW, have voluntarily imposed this upper limit rather than risk encouraging Germany's legislators finally to impose overall limits on the remaining unrestricted autobahns. Without this electronic conscience, the 500SL's ample power, high overall gearing and slippery shape would almost certainly take it closer to 170mph (274kph), but enough is enough . . .

ULTIMATE ACCOLADES

Long before the 500SL and family was launched, Mercedes had been taking orders at a quite remarkable rate from people who were willing to buy a £50,000-plus car, virtually sight-unseen, on the basis that it was a Mercedes and an SL. That is rare faith indeed. Admittedly, some were in the queue purely as part of the appalling late 1980s blight of 'investors' ordering cars long in advance, purely on the basis of knowing that

they would be in very short supply and therefore saleable immediately after launch to the highest bidder who had missed the waiting list.

As launched in Britain, SL prices ranged from £42,130 for the 12-valve six-cylinder 300SL, through £46,270 for the highly desirable 300SL-24, to £58,045 for the top-of-the-range 500SL. Within a few weeks, speculators were looking for anywhere between two and three times those figures for immediate delivery, and if you did not want to pay, the alternative was a wait which promised to stretch almost immediately to several years. Mercedes were as embarrassed as anyone by this unhappy state of affairs, and certainly did not encourage it, but in that they were only in a position to build some 20,000 cars a year they could hardly change it. Happily, a changing financial climate solved the problem for them, left some of the greedier speculators nursing deservedly burned fingers, brought demand more into line with supply and prices back to near those listed.

Hard as things became, Mercedes had few worries that the SL would struggle; quality simply continues to sell. And, of course, yet another ecstatic welcome for an SL line made the car's future success a certainty.

There were those (this author included) who suggested that the new SLs with all their electronic gadgetry, flip-up roll bars and unspeakably complex seats were a bit too clever for their own good, but no one ventured that in engineering terms they were anything less than a staggering achievement; and that still holds good. You can read details of driving the latest SLs elsewhere, but suffice to .say that the combination of world-beating chassis composure, magnificent engines, terrific performance and almost ultimate luxury and versatility marked this as the most completely accomplished SL yet. Some even said the most accomplished high-performance convertible yet.

Autocar & Motor's tester who brought us

*As part of the SL's dedication to safety, the seats are fully engineered units using
integrated belt-systems independent of the body; belt height adjusts to suit
head-rest height and there is an automatic tensioning system.*

into this chapter with his introductory comments was hard pushed to find cause to criticize. It was heavy, yes, and automatic transmission did not promise the best of performance, but no, the SL belied such thoughts with a 157mph (253kph) maximum, 0–60mph (0–97kph) in only 5.9 seconds and 0–100mph (0–161kph) in 14 seconds. The engine drew comparison with a Can-Am racer's for its sound and fury. The auto was the smoothest and fastest changing the magazine had ever encountered. Grip was enormous, control superb, and the ride fine and sporting. The steering drew some minus points for a lack of feel and the brakes

for being just not very good, but the finish, comfort and equipment impressed as expected – especially in the fully automated hard- and soft-top actions. There were minor niggles over head room and the usual over-firmness of the seats, and that even at this price air-conditioning and skid-control ought to be standard rather than extra-cost options. The conclusion was:

The 500SL has no real rivals; there simply isn't another car with its blend of attributes. Saloon car protection in a fully open car is a first.

The SL's road behaviour sets a standard

500SL, 1989–

Body type	:	two-door, two-seater roadster with powered folding soft-top and removable hard-top
Chassis	:	platform with unitary body
Engine type	:	90° V8
Capacity	:	4,973cc
Bore	:	96.5mm
Stroke	:	85.0mm
Compression ratio	:	10.0:1
Cylinders	:	alloy block, five main bearings
Cylinder head	:	alloy, four valves per cylinder operated by twin, chain-driven, overhead camshafts per cylinder bank, with variable inlet camshaft timing
Fuel system	:	Bosch KE5 CIS electronic injection
Maximum power	:	326bhp at 5,500rpm
Maximum torque	:	332lb ft at 4,000rpm
Bhp per litre	:	65.5
Gearbox type	:	four-speed automatic with torque converter and selectable modes
Gear ratios	:	Fourth: 1.00 Second: 2.25 Third: 1.44 First: 3.87 Reverse: 5.59
Final drive ratio	:	2.65:1
Clutch	:	n/a
Front suspension	:	strut type with lower wishbones, coil springs, telescopic gas-filled dampers, anti-roll bar
Rear suspension	:	multi-link, coil springs, telescopic gas-filled dampers, anti-roll bar, optional self-levelling control
Brakes	:	ventilated front discs with four-piston callipers, solid rear discs with two-piston callipers; servo assistance; ABS anti-lock system
Steering	:	recirculating ball, with power assistance
Wheels and tyres	:	alloy; 225/55ZR16 radial-ply tyres
Overall length	:	176.0in (447.0cm)
Overall width	:	71.3in (181.2cm)
Overall height	:	50.5in (129.3cm)
Wheelbase	:	99.0in (251.5cm)
Track	:	60.3in (153.2cm)
Ground clearance	:	6.0in (15.2cm)
Fuel tank capacity	:	21.1gal (80 litres)
Unladen weight	:	3,894lb (1,770kg)
Power to weight ratio	:	187.5bhp/ton

PERFORMANCE

Maximum speed	:	155mph (249kph) – artificially limited
0–60mph (0–97kph)	:	5.9sec
0–100mph (0–161kph)	:	14.0sec
Standing ¼ mile (0.4km)	:	14.4sec
Fuel consumption	:	approx 16mpg (5.7km per litre)

The roll-over bar can be left retracted during normal driving, but in the event of an accident it will spring into place within 0.3 seconds.

for powerful rear-drive cars, too. The optional acceleration skid control prevents car and driver getting into potentially dangerous situations, yet the chassis is thoroughly entertaining at the same time.

Safety and excitement go hand in hand in the SL, but it's the excitement a driver remembers; thrilling 157mph performance from the magnificent 326bhp, 32-valve V8, so ably assisted by the responsive and smooth four-speed automatic gearbox. Despite qualms about build quality and optional equipment that should be standard, we rate the 500SL as the world's greatest convertible, and one of the best sports cars, too.

Just over a year later, transplanted to *Performance Car*, the same tester, John Barker, chose the 500SL as his Car of the Year:

I decided that the two most desirable features were a V8 engine and rear-wheel drive (entertainment at both ends). The number of candidates quickly came down to a handful. A very expensive and exclusive handful granted, but it's not my fault that nobody makes a 2-litre V8 or that rear-drive cars under £20,000 are about as common as taxi drivers with change for a tenner ... the

Mercedes offers so many ways of enjoying motoring – cruising with hard top in place or with hood down, charging hard on twisting roads or slipping quietly down the motorway. Fun in safety for 365 days. The fact that it's got an automatic gearbox isn't really a cause for complaint; it's probably the best available and doesn't blunt the fabulous 48-valve V8's 326bhp. On the other hand, its sophisticated and effective traction control system would find itself decommissioned occasionally (simply by pulling a fuse). It doesn't hide any failing in the car's handling, as I know. And let's face it, a bit of oversteer in a well-sorted chassis is fun. I'm not a big fan of the SL's styling, I know it's ludicrously heavy and the electric hood is an extravagance. But the 500SL is massively entertaining.

Massively entertaining could possibly be the best way of summing up every SL that Mercedes ever built ...

There are more controls and more warning lights to monitor the state of numerous new electronic systems, but essentially, the SL is still a very sporty package.

9 Owning and Driving

With twenty or so completely distinct models (in six recognizably separate families) from the original 300SL coupé to the current 500SL, plus the options of detachable hard-tops, folding soft-tops or fixed-head coupés, the range of SLs and SLCs certainly lacks nothing in terms of variety.

Similarly, it offers a huge span of performance, and an equally broad span of prices for the potential owner. At the time of writing these range from as little as £5,000 for a tatty example of one of the less sought-after cars (for instance the SLCs, the smaller engined pagoda-roof series, and even the V8-generation 450SL) to as much as £250,000 for the best of the Gullwing 300SLs. Upper reaches for other models might currently be around £20,000 for a 190SL, a couple of thousand more for a 230 or 250SL, slightly less for the 280, and as little as £12,000 to £15,000 for even a very good example of a 350 or 450SL. In what has recently proved a notoriously volatile market, they have stayed steadier than most – probably reflecting the fact that broadly they are bought more for their value and quality than for their glamour.

In fact, between the demise of the first 300s and the arrival of the current generation, the SLs have kept a surprisingly low profile, yet they have always been very highly thought of in their day by testers and owners alike. Now, in the majority of cases at least, an SL (even one of the older ones) can provide perfectly practical everyday motoring, while still offering something of the classic experience. In every case the design and build quality, the standards of finish and equipment, and the long-term mechanical reliability are everything you would expect from a Mercedes, and in some cases the performance is even what you might expect from a sports car.

What is more, those typical selling prices can start to look very attractive indeed once you take into account the original price of the car as adjusted for inflation. At today's rates a 230 or 250SL even as launched, for instance, would cost approximately £30,000, a 450SL well over £42,000 with the SLC version over £52,000, or even the 'humble' 190SL at almost £30,000; in fact the only SLs which have significantly outstripped inflation are the 300SL Gullwing coupé and the 300SL Roadster – equating to around £48,000 and £54,000 respectively at today's prices yet in the very best cases valued at over four times more. Investment might not be the best reason for buying an everyday car, but if anything the majority of SLs do seem to offer remarkable value with practicality.

SOUND AND SIMPLE

Given so many models, the comments in this short appraisal can only be brief and general out of necessity, but it can be said with reasonable certainty that the vast majority of SLs are not cars to be frightened of if they should need work to bring them back to their best. Compared to more overtly exotic models, all the SLs (with the possible exceptions of the earliest 300s and the latest high-tech generation) are really quite simple cars mechanically, and blessed with the strength of quality engineering.

Many of the basic items of running gear were used in other, more common models, and so remain quite easily available (at a price), but their underlying design strength makes it unusual for many items to be completely beyond rescue anyway. Mercedes philosophy has always been to build engines and running gear that last, and in that respect the SLs are outstandingly robust, with what might seem an extraordinarily high mileage in an ordinary car being barely the flush of youth in a Mercedes. This style-to-last tradition also means that (given the eye of the beholder) any SL still does look very special.

Finally, even if the company continued to insist on calling them sports cars, the majority of owners did not treat them as such, so it is really quite rare to find an SL that has been mechanically extended to a serious degree – rather the opposite if anything, as Mercedes tend to be well cared for if only to preserve the image. It is, of course, always worth insisting on a car with a service history that is as full as possible, always making sure that all the hard- and soft-top options are still with the car, and always remembering that prices for spares are more likely to reflect the 1990's market than the 1950's or 1960's one. That said, and so long as you are realistic about restoration and running costs, an SL need not threaten any horrors.

STARTING AT THE TOP

In this case, starting at the beginning in most respects means starting at the top; the original Gullwing is amongst the fastest of the SLs even if you include the current ones, definitely among the rarest and most desirable, and predictably amongst the most valuable. As a consequence, most of the survivors are either in the well-preserved-original or fully-restored categories, and are used by enthusiast owners. In this condition they offer few serious worries beyond routine maintenance – things will wear in time but it is very unusual for anything to

break – so it is a car which can still be enjoyed to the full.

Up to a point, the 300SL coupé is an easy car to drive, and even quite a practical tourer. The experience starts, of course, with climbing in, but that is not as difficult as some would suggest. The gullwing doors open easily on their counterbalance struts, open very high and leave a generous hole in the roof. The steering wheel also folds flat via one simple knob on the column and then you only have to negotiate the high, wide sills. In fact, the sills give you a well-padded intermediate seat on which to place your bottom while you swing your legs into the cockpit.

Once inside, the coupé is comfortable, light and airy, with a good deal more glass than many contemporaries. The seats are wide but well shaped and supportive. Except for the inevitable huge wheel, the driving position is tolerably straight-armed and modern, and although all the dashboard's chrome and paint give the instruments a distinctly period feel, they are comprehensive, well laid out and easy to read – this was, after all, only one step removed from a real racing car. On the other hand, it actually has quite reasonable luggage space behind the seats (especially if you have the fitted luggage that Mercedes offered), and has pretty good heating and ventilation. The side windows do not wind down but they are easily removable and can be stowed in a neat bag. The fresh air throughput and heater are effective in all but the worst heat – the generous glass area can act like a greenhouse in the sunshine, but with the big engine ahead there are rarely any problems in cold weather.

The 300SL is still a 1950's car, of course. Although it is injected, there is a manual 'choke' for cold starting, plus the auxiliary pump switch and even a timing adjuster, but in most cases only the ignition and starter switch are needed. The engine is smooth and docile at low speeds, with massive flexibility,

The dash of the 190SL is just as elegant as its big brother's, and with similarly thoughtful touches like the individual heater controls for driver and passenger.

naturally, but a surprisingly well-muted growl; only at much higher speeds is it more intrusive, and then with a wonderful, hard scream confirming its racing background. Even by modern standards, the power and especially the torque are enormously impressive.

Nor is it a particularly demanding car in normal driving. Clutch and brake pedals are quite heavy, but firm and progressive; the steering is *very* heavy at low speeds, but that is the penalty of only two turns between locks and it does lighten up markedly at higher speeds while retaining excellent feel. The gear-change is light and easy to use, in a positive gate and with synchromesh on all four forward gears. The ratios are nicely spaced, although in any case the power is so well spread that the car is very forgiving of those who do not enjoy stirring the lever. If

there is one fault with the car in terms of user comfort, it is the very intrusive high-pitched transmission noise, which can be tiresome and tiring on a long drive.

The straight-line performance is still highly impressive, with solid and relentless acceleration on tap right up to very high speeds, and also with superb stability. The balance, of course, depends on which final drive option is fitted – low ratios give acceleraton at the expense of top speed, higher ratios vice versa, as described earlier.

The ride reflects Uhlenhaut's philosophy of stiff chassis with supple, long-travel springing and firm damping. It is actually quite comfortable on all but the worst surfaces at low speeds, though there is always plenty of feedback from the road.

The downside of the suspension is now legendary, and unfortunately the legend is true. Up to a point, the 300SL coupé handles quite precisely and predictably, but on relatively narrow cross-ply tyres the grip is strictly limited; and worse than that, the swing-axle's camber and roll-centre changes can make the transition from neutral to oversteer frighteningly abrupt; either from going into a corner too quickly under power or even more worryingly from the 'natural' reaction of lifting off the power abruptly when near the limits of adhesion. The approved technique for rapid progress is slow into corners with just sufficient power on, then steadily increasing acceleration through and out, to make the most of the traction without aggravating the geometry. Just remember that this is a car that rewards skill but can punish ineptitude or indecision.

One other thing, brakes that were widely remarked as among the best in the world in the mid-1950s would strike most people as strictly marginal now in a car with the 300SL's performance. They work best when they are hot, but they always need a firm push, and they do fade . . .

As for the Roadster, it overcame several of the coupé's worst tendencies. With its improved rear axle layout and later disc brakes, it was usefully more forgiving (if still not without its vices); and with its 'proper' doors and more usable boot space it was even more practical. However, it was heavier, a bit slower and in spite of its soft-top/hard-top versatility, never quite so glamorous – hence the unusual situation of an open-topped car which is (marginally) less sought after now than its solid-roofed equivalent.

BABY BROTHER

Ironically only a little less scarce than the 300s these days is the other end of the SL spectrum, the four-cylinder 190SL. Several things account for the smaller number of survivors. As a less powerful car it had less

in reserve and often tended to be driven harder in compensation, and it was in some ways a complex and awkward car to work on, so with maintenance costs somewhat out of proportion to the low initial cost, it was more likely to be neglected. Also, being the first generation of Mercedes' unit body, the 190SL's shell had a serious vulnerability to attack by rust.

The latter is the worst problem for a 190SL now – it can, after all be over thirty-five years old, and Mercedes did not apply any rust prevention in the early days of unit construction. An untreated 190 can rust pretty well anywhere except in the doors, boot and bonnet lids (which were aluminium). Parts of the floor and inner wings were double-skinned and as such were particularly prone to trapped water, but everything from the sills and jacking points to the rear spring top mounts could provide terminal problems. Repairs are possible, of course, but that can be horribly expensive now that most original panels are unavailable.

Mechanically, if the car has survived this far then it should not present big problems. Although the four-cylinder engine only has three main bearings, it is strong and reliable so long as it is properly looked after – though parts are now generally expensive. Like most, it tends to show wear first in the timing chain and the valve guides, and the interface between alloy head and iron block can cause just as many corrosion and overheating problems in a Mercedes as it does in any lesser car. It is an awkward engine to work on when it is *in situ*, with too many of the ancillaries buried under the complicated carburettor assembly – and if that needs replacing, it is a very expensive job indeed. Even the manual gearbox needs a special oil because the tolerances within are so fine.

That said, the 190SL is surprisingly true to the SL philosophy and still offers an attractively sporty package for a small fraction of the cost of its more potent contemporaries. It has the versatility of soft- and hard-tops, and is comfortable and acceptably roomy for two – or three at a pinch with its transverse rear 'seat'.

It is not, of course, a quick car by modern standards (in fact it was not really a quick car even in its day) but what it lacks in performance it largely makes up for with character. If it was a 'cheap' Mercedes, it was still a Mercedes, and that reflects in the build quality and the fittings. Inside, a 190SL does not give away a great deal to a 300SL Roadster in terms of ambience, which was a deliberate ploy to make the most of the association.

If the 1.9-litre engine is not especially powerful, it is at least willing to rev towards the 6,000rpm mark, and so long as the notoriously difficult twin Solex carburettor set-up is properly in tune it is surprisingly refined for a fairly big four – but then it is a Mercedes.

It is probably at its best for cruising, but within the limits of only around 120bhp in a car weighing substantially over a ton, it is admirably flexible too and in its day was considered to be quite a slogger for an engine with such a high specific output. Slogging is not performance, though, and to achieve that, the engine preferred to be kept on the boil. The closer ratio gearbox that Mercedes added soon after the 190SL's launch helps in that respect, and most testers advocated using it to the full to make the most of the modest power. The change was occasionally remarked as being a little notchy and tight, but in general it was considered a good gearbox and the 190 was fine as an 80mph (129kph) cruiser with a 0–60mph (0–97kph) time in the region of 12 seconds.

It was comfortable, with typically generous Mercedes seats, a compliant ride and equipment levels not far short of the big cars – including the excellent heating and ventilation system with individual adjustment.

On the road it was considered agile and very safe, with the low-pivot axle, remember, to make it rather less skittish than the contemporaneous Gullwing. It had 3½ turns of steering lock and was a lot lighter anyway, so it did not take muscle to drive a 190SL and it would understeer before it would oversteer, which was not something the big car was often accused of. Being lighter also gave the brakes an easier time and although smaller wheels had forced smaller diameter drums on the car, they were wide and finned and pretty well up to the job. All in all, it was and is quite an attractive car for its purpose.

PAGODA TOPS

Inevitably, the pagoda-topped second generation, as a replacement for the 300 and 190SLs, was considered a compromise at the time, but it soon won its spurs.

Today it is old enough to have more in common with the first generation 'classics' where the later V8s are maybe more identifiable with the current cars, but again, it is a perfectly usable car today.

The 230SL perhaps has the tamest image of all the bigger SLs, but it also has a reputation as one of the best balanced and most genuinely sporty cars of the whole series – combining just about enough power with what for its day was quite outstanding chassis behaviour and the usual SL qualities of comfort and style. The options of power steering and automatic transmission (taken up by the majority of buyers) took away most of the effort but little of the underlying character, and (whatever the purists said) they actually suited the car very well. Less successful was the slightly fussy trim, the stylized dashboard with its odd vertical instruments, and the fact that although it was bigger, the car was still only a marginal two plus two. Its versatility was a bonus though, and both hard- and soft-tops were superbly finished and totally weatherproof.

As ever, the rules are that you should buy

the best you can afford, insist on a service history, and be prepared to spend money on proper maintenance and upkeep. Like the earlier cars, this series is generally reliable mechanically, though compromised on early models by those very short service intervals. There was some tendency to timing chain wear, and out-of-tune injection can make a basically sound engine seem very much worse than it actually is, but expert tuning works wonders. Brakes and dampers, too, have a harder time with the heavier car, but these are maintenance problems rather than ones that will render the car unserviceable.

Although not as bad as in the 190SL, rust is a potential problem everywhere except in the alloy panels of some cars. It can attack the front wings and arches, the boot floor and the front and rear undertrays. Rust in the sills may only be in the removable outer covers, and if there is a serious problem it is likely to be in the rear chassis legs. That said, the 'pagoda' shells are really very robust and/or reasonable to repair, so it is rarely necessary to write one off completely through corrosion. Remember again though that this car could now be nearly thirty years old, and not everything comes off the shelf any more.

The big attraction is that it is still so usable. In general, the story is that the later cars have the power while the early ones, with their firmer suspension bushings, have the sharpness – otherwise little was changed.

Nowadays a 280SL, for instance, is far from disgraced as a sporty tourer – a real *grand* tourer, in fact, in the old sense. With 170bhp and better gearing it was the most potent of the series and consequently the one that needed to be worked least hard. It was actually quite quick in the lower reaches at the expense of being a bit frenetic at really high speeds, but the combination is attractive and it will still cruise all day at something over 100mph (161kph). As so often on German cars with their tendency to a low bottom gear and 'autobahn' top gear, the intermediate ratios are rather widely spaced, but the four-speed automatic with fluid coupling is at least very quick and responsive. It is almost best considered as a two-pedal manual, giving you the option of proper hands-off cruising or flicking the slim, chrome lever through the neat gate if you want to drive more enthusiastically.

The most notable advance with this series though, was its handling on the specially developed radial tyres. You need only look at the wide, squat stance of the car to know that this was where so much of the work went, and it shows on the road. With wishbones at the front and the low-pivot swing axle with roll-compensating spring and torque arms, it is comfortable and well behaved. It rolls very little, and although the rear-end transition is ultimately still there, it comes at much higher limits and with much more warning. With the proviso that the nose really does dip quite badly under heavy braking, the brakes are also excellent, and all in all, the pagoda-top SLs are very sporty indeed.

TOWARDS LUXURY

In spite of more cylinders, more capacity, more power and ultimately more performance, the V8 generation is more about luxury and comfort than about real sportiness; pay your money and take your choice.

Being more recent, they are less trouble even than the commendably hassle-free older SLs in some respects. The shells, for instance, are the most rust-resistant of all (and even more so from the late 1970s when new manufacturing and protection methods were introduced). If the bug does strike, it will be in the familiar areas of arches, sills, rear chassis and boot floor. Even in the unlikely event that rust has really taken hold, most panels are still readily available – this model, after all, was only finally dropped as recently as 1989. By the same token, more or less all mechanical parts come over the counter, so running a V8-generation SL need be little more complicated than running any recent model, high-quality car.

In this case, quality was the operative word; these were very quick SLs, especially in European trim and with the big all-alloy engines, but Mercedes emphasized the comfort and refinement ahead of the performance.

Safety and environmental consciousness had made them heavy, but the heaviness showed itself as an incomparable solidity and quality of furnishing and fitting. The interiors were finally a lot more conventional and as beautifully finished and fully equipped as any expensive saloon's, with superb leather, thick carpets and wood – the latter, it might be said, not to everyone's taste. They were almost without exception automatics, but again Mercedes' autos were amongst the best in the world and the easy option thoroughly suited the sybaritic nature of the cars – although those who would have taken manuals given the option were apt to call them stodgy or lethargic.

The V8s had few critics. They are magnificent engines, massively flexible and amply powerful yet extremely refined and full of sporty character. Do not expect them to be frugal though; in spite of the public relations lip-service to the fuel crisis, they are very far from that, especially when used with any enthusiasm.

If you so choose, these cars really can be used that way. The chassis was more solid than ever and by this stage the suspension was exceptionally refined, with the most sophisticated of rear layouts and full anti-dive and anti-squat geometry built in to answer the recurring criticisms of the pagoda-roof cars. The combination of limousine ride and sporting grip and handling was possibly the best yet, though it has to be said that it lacks the entertainment value and lightness of touch of the best pagoda-topped cars, and could hardly disguise the ever-increasing weight and bulk of the cars.

Fortunately, the power steering was another of Mercedes' most attractive features, doing the job without ever being intrusive or denying the driver proper feel of the road and car. The brakes were simply exceptional, well up to stopping such a heavy car repeatedly and undramatically, even from the 140mph (225kph) or so that a 500SL was capable of. If the first generation of V8 SLs had a problem in life, it was that by the late 1980s they had been around for a very long time, and that even when they had arrived they had been seen as something of a continuation of what went before. Now, of course, we can just think of it as a classic.

TODAY'S SLs

As for the latest generation, it is recent enough for buying second-hand to be virtually the same as buying new, but the driving experience has put a lot of the performance back alongside even more luxury and technology. The author described the 500SL experience in *Fast Lane* magazine in May 1990:

That begins with slipping open the flick-knife-like key and zapping the electronic locking, which responds with a twinkling green light on the door handle for open, a twinkling red for locked.

Once inside, you can get comfortable either with the excellent Mercedes 'model-seat' switches and the electric column adjustment, or by hitting your choice of three memory buttons which adjust not only the seat but also the column *and* the rear-view mirror. It doesn't mop your brow for the effort, however . . .

The engine is glorious. Thoroughbred V8, four chain-driven cams, 32 valves, big German horses. It has everything, from rustling tickover through almost uncannily quiet cruising ability to thunderous high-speed performance. Thank God Mercedes didn't silence out all the fun. It feels strong throughout the range, smooth and potent with absolutely instant, linear throttle response, and it is handsomely matched by the four-speed automatic . . .

The ratios have to be excellent. Fair enough, there's 326bhp here and 332lb ft of widely spread torque, but the *Sport Licht* isn't all that *Licht* any more when it comes to the scales. At 34.8cwt kerb weight it weighs very nearly the same as two XR2is, and musters 187bhp/ton, which is somewhere around mid-911 territory and just a touch short of a 928. That said, it wasn't quite as quick for us as it's supposed to be: 0–60 averaged 6.4sec, 0–100 15sec; using Economy added 0.3 to 60 and a mere tenth to 100, for what it's worth. The intermediate kickdown times are impressive enough, 2.7sec from 40 to 60; three seconds dead from 50 to 70; five dead from 80 to 100; and just 7.1 from 100 to 120. This is v quick.

And the maximum? Ah, thereby hangs a tale. In theory it is artificially governed to 155mph by the appropriate chip, but in practice it was governed shortly before that by our man with the iron nerves and sophisticated stopwatch opting for self-preservation

A nice, tidy interior on a 420SL that obviously serves for everyday use. Wood, leather and carpets all look sound. Optional rear seats are strictly 'occasional'.

rather than a few more clicks on Millbrook's high-speed bowl. In his own words 'The car gets very loose at high speed, which seems to be an aerodynamic problem. At an indicated 155mph round Millbrook I decided to chicken out, because life is too short . . .' This from the man who does not know the meaning of the word 'fear', so I am not about to suggest doing better . . .

Alas, the feedback from the road in other respects is less easy to find. The SL is actually more compact than it looks, at just 14ft 9in long and on a 99in wheelbase, and basically it has exceptionally good handling; a small amount of rear-wheel compliance toe-in, mainly through compression of the lower control arm bushes on spring compression, makes for a basic mild understeerer, which the SL is up to very high limits. At higher speeds it is all but neutral, unless you get into plough-on mode on very slick surfaces, which we managed just once to a serious degree. It is eventually *just* possible to force oversteer by going into a quick corner too quickly and too deeply (just, that is, without falling off), but that is oversteer from the momentum of the back trying to overtake the front.

The other sort – power oversteer generated by sacrificing the lateral grip of the rear tyres to tractive effort from giving it some wellie – ain't on in the anti-wheelspin-equipped SL. Try to boot it and the ABS sensors detect the onset of the inner wheel spinning, the brake goes on and the motor throttles back while you lament the denial of a big opposite lock moment. Don't go for a handbrake turn either, not unless you're Jake the Peg; the SL has a nasty US-type foot parking brake . . .

For all this hard-to-fathom blend of excellence and frustration, you will pay a basic price of £58,045 (or at least you would if you were at the front of the queue now and didn't have to face a three-year wait). On top of that, to get to the spec as tested you can add £307.43 for the cruise control, £1,263.98 for the airbag, £1,820.34 for the Acceleration Skid Control, £1,109.92 for the rear child seats, £2,002.25 for the (brilliant) air conditioning, and £365.52 for the front seat heating. That's £64,914.44 altogether – £6,869.64 in extras, enough in itself to buy you a wide choice from the basic range Unos, Fiestas, Metros, Novas or R5s; even a basic Peugeot 205. If you want a pre-owned one to beat the queue, it will be a lot more than that; funny old world, innit?

So what does it come to at the end of the day? Well, maybe the 500SL is the best of all kinds of things – the most refined, the best equipped (or at least the most cleverly equipped), the most sybaritic, but it doesn't necessarily add up to the most exciting. Don't misunderstand, it is exceptional in so many ways, the performance is massively impressive, the roadholding is of a very high order, the handling is near idiot-proof, and the luxury and twin-top versatility are real. It's even sporty in an Ascot Royal enclosure sort of way, but it isn't a true sports car, not like the blurb says . . .

But chuck away the tricks, and the excess weight with them, keep the fabulous basics but involve the driver more in exploiting them, let it be what it is crying out to be from under the pomposity, and it could be truly unbelievable. Put me down for the 32-valve 560SL Sport Equipment . . .

All that, believe it or not, was actually the sort of compliment that testers have been paying the SLs for almost four decades. I have driven several examples since that first meeting and grown to understand it more and more. Maybe it is still a bit over the top if you're really expecting an out-and-out sports car, and maybe a no-frills model with even more power *would* re-create the ultimate thrill of the earliest 300SL Gullwings (in the unlikely event that Mercedes ever chose to build such a thing), but in the meantime the SL tradition looks safe for its entry into the twenty-first century.

Index